SALE PRICE

SCHOOL OF ORIENTAL AND AFRICAN STUDIES

UNIVERSITY OF LONDON

Jordan Lectures in Comparative Religion

XI

The Louis H. Jordan Bequest

The will of the Rev. Louis H. Jordan provided that the greater part of his estate should be paid over to the School of Oriental and African Studies to be employed for the furtherance of Studies in Comparative Religion, to which his life had been devoted. Part of the funds which thus became available was to be used for the endowment of a Louis H. Jordan Lectureship in Comparative Religion. The lecturer is required to deliver a course of six or eight lectures for subsequent publication. The first series of lectures was delivered in 1951.

JORDAN LECTURES 1974

Beyond Tradition and Modernity

Changing Religions in a Changing World

by

R. J. ZWI WERBLOWSKY

The Hebrew University of Jerusalem

UNIVERSITY OF LONDON

THE ATHLONE PRESS

1976

Published by
THE ATHLONE PRESS
UNIVERSITY OF LONDON
at 4 *Gower Street London* WC1
Distributed by Tiptree Book Services Ltd
Tiptree, Essex

USA and Canada
Humanities Press Inc
New Jersey

© *School of Oriental and African Studies* 1976

0 485 17411 1

Printed in Great Britain by
T. & A. CONSTABLE LTD
EDINBURGH

For JONATHAN, NAʿAMAH, NOAM, NAVAH *and* JESSICA
heirs, victims and re-makers of both tradition and modernity

PREFACE

The present little book contains the text of the Louis H. Jordan Lectures in Comparative Religion in essentially the form in which they were delivered at the School of Oriental and African Studies (University of London) in June 1974. Only minor alterations were made in the process of converting words spoken to an audience into a text addressed to a reading public (e.g., the disappearance of 'Mr Chairman, Ladies and Gentlemen', or the substitution of 'chapter' wherever the original version said 'lecture'). It is in the nature of all formal occasions, including public university lectures, to be subject to the constraints—or rather the straitjacket—of time, and hence several paragraphs contained in the written version had to be omitted from the oral presentation. For the same reason the elaboration of certain (at times quite essential) points as well as references to certain current discussions had to be relegated to the notes at the end of the volume.

Any attempt at discussing the roles and developments of religions in the present age courts the dangers of superficiality, hasty generalization, and undue reliance on secondary sources. The author does not for a moment entertain the illusion of having avoided, let alone withstood these dangers. Perhaps the major contribution this book can hope to make is to have others profit from its mistakes and thereby help them produce more reliable and substantial studies. The author is grateful to the many friends, colleagues and writers on whose work he has drawn, sometimes to the point of plagiarism. A special word of apology is due to all those scholars whose insights and contributions I have so successfully 'internalized' that I have failed to recognize their origin and hence also to make due acknowledgement. The bibliography at the end of the volume lists works that have been quoted or referred to in the text or notes; it does not pretend to be in any way exhaustive. Fortunately many of the titles listed contain very full bibliographies on their subject-matter.

The reader should bear in mind that this is not a book on Christianity, Judaism, Islam etc. It is a survey of religion in the situation loosely described as 'modernity'. Hence certain phenomena are discussed where such a discussion seemed appropriate, although the same phenomena or set of problems could equally well have been treated under the heading of another religion. I have tried to mitigate this extremely misleading though inevitable appearance of rigid divisions by means of cross-references as well as—alas—some repetitiousness. Thus, e.g., some of the observations pertinent to a discussion of Judaism have been made in the chapter on Islam, whilst some considerations relevant to modern Islam (e.g., the ambivalence towards modernity due to the 'Western' origins of the latter) will be found in the chapter on Hinduism and Buddhism. In fact every chapter deals with problems that are relevant to each and every religion. The choice of the context for the fuller elaboration of any particular point was, more often than not, a matter of convenience.

I am deeply grateful to The School of Oriental and African Studies in the University of London for having done me the signal honour of inviting me to deliver the 1974 series of The Louis H. Jordan Lectures in Comparative Religion. The hospitality extended by the Dean of the School, Professor Ch. von Fürer-Haimendorf; the kindness shown by my many friends and colleagues; and last but not least the unobtrusively courteous help offered by the office of the Secretary, all combined to make this series of Jordan Lectures a memorable experience at least for the lecturer.

The final version of the present work was written out during a sabbatical leave from the Hebrew University of Jerusalem, most of which was spent as a Visiting Fellow at The Netherlands Institute for Advanced Studies in the Humanities and Social Sciences (NIAS) in Wassenaar, during the academic year 1973/4. Whatever virtues this modest little study may possess are largely due to the pleasant working conditions and the congenial atmosphere at NIAS. The shortcomings, alas, are the author's own.

London, June 1974   R. J. Zwi Werblowsky

CONTENTS

I
Secularization and Secularism:
Cultural Process and Ideological Critique

The series of lectures presented in this book constitutes, possibly as a tribute to modernity, a departure from the venerable tradition of Louis H. Jordan Lectures in Comparative Religion. Under the terms of the Jordan Bequest, the lecturer was to institute 'a searching comparison between not more than two religions' and then to tabulate his findings in 'a carefully detailed and comprehensive manner'. The present series deals with a subject that hardly admits of detailed and comprehensive findings. We shall try to compare—if comparison is the right word—two types of religion, often referred to as traditional or pre-modern on the one hand, and post-traditional, modern or even post-modern on the other. This dubious generalization, in its turn, implies another even more dubious one, to wit, that we can speak of religion in the singular and not only of religions in the plural. For surely if we want to speak of Christianity, Islam or Buddhism (and these too are generalizing abstractions the legitimacy of which has been contested) not simply by way of comparing and/or contrasting their doctrines, practices, social dimensions and cultural and spiritual styles, but by focussing more specifically on their critical transitions into and beyond modernity, then an awful lot is being taken for granted. Let me therefore, in order to obviate misunderstandings, state quite plainly at the outset some of the basic assumptions made, perhaps somewhat too dogmatically and uncritically, by at least one impenitent practitioner of the Comparative Study of Religions. Comparative Religionists are professional neo-Lutherans: even if they do not have the strength to sin boldly, at least they cannot help erring boldly. Their motto is: *erra fortiter*.

My first assumption is that we do not have to define religion in order to talk about it. A great many definitions have been proposed, some of them very useful but none of them really adequate. In the circumstances you will bear with me if I do not propose to make a fool of myself in public by suggesting yet another inadequate definition. Some of the better known definitions are so wide as to include too much—with the result that we are spending a great deal of time on such academic parlour games as discussing whether the so-called secular ideologies should or should not be called 'secular religions', 'substitute religions', or 'functional equivalents' of religion. Other definitions again are so narrow as to exclude important phenomena—as has happened, e.g., when theistic theologians in earlier days insisted on describing Theravada-Buddhism as a philosophy rather than a religion.[1] Some definitions have proved extremely helpful, especially when they did not pretend to be exhaustive, let alone prescriptive, but merely served an operational purpose, or as indicators of the general direction to which a particular study or investigation was oriented. Few anthropologists, however faulty their formal definitions of religion, ever had difficulties in distinguishing between a ritual and a secular dance (whatever the ritual elements present even in the latter). We all start out with a vague notion of what religion is, carefully feeling our way, or perhaps smelling it with our noses, rather than clearly seeing with our eyes, in the hope that as we toil along the mists will lift and our subject matter assume more definite outlines. Our intuitions as well as our analytical results, our subjective as well as our allegedly more objective insights, will have to be constantly checked and re-checked against the intuitions, analytical results and insights of other scholars whose cultural biases and individual blind spots may help to neutralize and cancel out our own. Comparative Religion, perhaps more than any other branch of cross-cultural study, is a corporate undertaking.

I shall not review or discuss here the definitions of religion which I have found to be most helpful (Geertz 1966; Spiro

[1] In all fairness it should be noted that such narrowness of definition was not the exclusive prerogative of Christian philosophers. It was shared by a number of Buddhist 'modernists'; see below, p. 83.

1966; van Baaren 1973). The reader is undoubtedly familiar with them and I shall, therefore, address myself to my immediate theme. Something seems to have happened to the world, including its religions, which makes us grope for words in an effort to clarify and interpret to ourselves, and for ourselves, what it is that has happened. Having said that much, I have already stated the ambiguity of our undertaking. For to interpret is to try to make sense of something. And since man is an animal that tries to make sense of things, even the most scholarly and objective intentions have their ideological functions (if not purposes).[1] As a result we come up with an at times confusing vocabulary. The spectrum ranges from 'enlightened' (in eighteenth-century Europe) to post-modern (in the twentieth-century West), with secular, secularized, rational, 'disenchanted', scientific, modern, modernizing, post-traditional and the like occupying any number of points along this line. This vocabulary, when prudently, responsibly and critically handled has proved exceedingly illuminating in much recent study. But it is no less illuminating —albeit for very different reasons—also when used, as is all too often the case, in a variety of confused and confusing ways. However, before enlarging on that, let me state as clearly as I can my own cultural bias and intellectual blind spots, and this not only by way of methodological apology but also because it is germane to the very nature of our subject.

It is nowadays taken for granted that there always has been change. It is not the fact of change that is under discussion, but our scientific and cultural attitudes to this fact. By scientific attitude I mean the conceptual tools evolved by the appropriate historical and social sciences to describe, measure and explain change. By cultural attitudes I mean the sort of statement made, e.g., at the beginning of this paragraph: 'it is nowadays taken for granted that there always has been change'. In fact, we take it so much for granted that we only enquire whether change is slow or fast, partial or integral and pervasive, conscious or

---

[1] It is unnecessary to draw attention once more to the truism that 'function' and 'purpose' are not the same; for a fuller discussion see D. Emmet (1958).

unconscious. The latter dichotomy is of particular interest, since it assumes that whilst all cultures and societies exhibit change, they do not all in equal measure affirm it. Some cultures may even pretend to ignore it. Traditional religions have often tended to deny the extent of historical change of which they were, and are, the living witnesses and embodiments, pretending that their present shape was the original, unadulterated article. When forced to recognize the facts of historical change, they would try to draw its sting by claiming this change to have been the legitimate unfolding of the religion's implicit character and essential nature. If change had to be actively desired or brought about, then a previous, negative change was assumed (corruption, degeneracy) and the new change legitimated as a 'reforming' movement in the sense of a return to the pristine, undefiled truth. As we shall see in the course of our survey, this is precisely the method adopted by many so-called 'modernist' movements. Practically all religions have known the kind of traditionalism that was opposed—in theory at least—to all innovative change: *sit ut est, aut non sit*. Hence the instinctive fear among many traditionalists of the destructive impact on religion of the historical sciences which would force upon them the awareness of change. Historical study has, in fact, been one of the weapons of criticism—a weapon that was gladly adopted by some schools of religious modernism since it could provide confirmation and legitimation of continuing change. The degree of 'tradition orientedness' of a religious culture determines to a great extent the nature of its encounter with modernity and the ways in which it handles the dialectics of rejection, appropriation and integration. Over and against the conservative functions of religious traditions, the history of religions also knows utopian and 'revolutionary' forms of eschatology and messianism. Their role in processes of change, and especially as religious precursors of later secularized legitimations of radical change, is a commonplace that does not require detailed comment here. What should be stressed in the present context is that also radical forms of eschatology usually try to legitimate themselves by appeal to one or more elements of tradition. With E. Shils (1971, pp. 144 f.), we should regard rejection, innovation and even revolt as new emphases on hitherto 'marginal' strands of tradition. Every New Testament, so to speak, appeals to the authority of an Old Testament in order to legitimate itself as being 'according to the scriptures'.

It is, therefore, of paramount importance to study not only the actual processes of change, but also the images of change (viz. the presence or absence of such images) in the various cultures. And here, alas, the borderline between what I called cultural and scientific attitudes begins to blur. Since science is an aspect of culture this does not come as a surprise. The question why certain branches and methods of study evince a preoccupation with the problem of change whereas others—e.g., some forms of structuralism—do not, is as much a matter of cultural style as of scientific methodology. Surely Lévi-Strauss' distinction between 'hot' and 'cold' history, whilst undoubtedly a brilliant *bon mot*, does not take us very far. Conversely, interest in change may be more than just a choice of research preference; it can be a commitment to the process itself. In fact, the word 'change' oscillates between a scientific-conceptual and a politico-ideological function much as do other key terms figuring in our discussion (e.g. 'secularization', 'modernization').

At this point it will be necessary to let the cat, or rather two cats, out of the bag. Not only the language (which happens to be English) in which we discuss our subject as well as our whole conceptual apparatus, but also the historical experience and perspective from which we construct the reality to be analysed are typically Western. They are the very flesh and bones of Western culture. No doubt this may render everything I shall have to say extremely parochial. To cap it all, I unabashedly intend to be parochial with a vengeance by assuming that the source, or at least the catalyst of most of the developments experienced by most contemporary societies and cultures as constituting the very stuff of the 'modern' crisis, has been the impact of the West. This impact has generally had the character of an invasion;

not only military, economic and colonial invasion, but also invasion of ideas, values and cultural patterns to be admired and emulated, or rejected and repudiated with greater or lesser degrees of vehemence and with stronger or weaker combinations of ambivalent love-hate, and to be adopted and adapted by means of conscious and unconscious selective mechanisms operating on diverse levels of awareness, make-believe, unwitting assimilation and at times apologetic, at times aggressive rationalization ranging from the naïve to the glib and at times even intellectually fraudulent.

In adopting a parochially Western point of departure I mean to suggest that in the West a number of things have happened that appear to be of decisive significance for the rest of the world, and that Western religion has undergone changes that are, to some extent, paradigmatic for all other religions. What I very emphatically do not say, and do not wish to be misunderstood as saying, is that Western experience sets the standard by which all other developments have to be measured. Even less do I wish to suggest a theory of the necessary and inevitable transcultural or intercultural convergence on the Western model of all modern social developments. This would be patently untrue even in the economic sphere, let alone in other social and cultural domains. Industrialization—whatever its relationship to, and functional interrelation with 'modernization'—has clearly taken a different course from its Western parent model in many industrializing and modernizing societies (cf. Feldman and Moore 1965). In fact, my point at present is precisely the very distinctive character of the Western experience, and the very obvious paradox deriving from this experience. The aforementioned colonial, imperialist, economic, missionary and cultural invasion, in both its aggressive and its less overtly aggressive forms, was the result of dynamisms generated and released by Western culture. Since this is not a symposium on Max Weber, I do not have to ask here why by Western culture and not by others. One of the decisive features of this culture was an increasingly reflective self-awareness, criticism and objectivation. Not only the sciences (about which Weber unfortunately said too little) and technology, but also the sense of history and the consciousness of change (both as a process in which one takes part and as an object of systematic study and analysis) are hallmarks of Western modernity. The modern sense of history imposes maximum objectivation also as regards the models and paradigms of tradition, including that aspect of tradition that makes it the guardian of the 'sacredness' and authority of cultural models and paradigms. Hence also the social and historical sciences were forged on the anvil of Western modernity before being 'applied' to other cultures. As a result we find ourselves in an awkward quandary. Western scientists have examined the bodies of presumably Western men and women, and have discovered the nature of the circulation of the blood or the function of certain glands. Yet we presume that their discoveries hold true of all men, and that inoculation against smallpox benefits all societies, and nobody is accused of Western ethnocentrism because of this presumption. However when we speak of, e.g., secularization, we are referring to a specific process in Western history since the eighteenth century, and the question arises whether the term can legitimately be applied to other cultures or whether it is an illegitimate extrapolation from one very particular historical experience. I suggest that the answer, however paradoxical it may seem, should be an affirmation of both statements. Our concepts are indeed derived from Western experience, and yet they can be used—provided we do so with much prudence, plenty of qualifications and continuous critical testing—when analysing other cultures precisely because the Western paradigm is relevant for them too. As I have said before, it is not a question of approximating or conforming to a Western standard, but of recognizing the role and significance of the Western paradigm not only as a causative factor but also as a convenient reference point for comparison that may throw into greater relief the characteristics of other cultures in responding to Western impact and influences. Response here means not only how societies change and adapt

B

under this impact, but also the ways in which they transform that which *prima facie* they seem to adopt, and not infrequently adopt that which they *prima facie* appear to reject, by bringing to bear upon it their own resources.

We shall therefore deal with a range of different yet similar problems in a number of religions. It is my contention that contemporary developments in these religions cannot be understood without a prior understanding of the Western impact. To assert this is not to lodge a claim for an inherent superiority of the West or to defend the equation modernization = Westernization (about which something will have to be said later). After all we also speak of the decisive role of Hellenism for the civilization of the Roman Empire, or that of Greek philosophy for medieval Western theology, or that of China for the civilization of Japan, without feeling apologetic about it. The fact of the matter is that the West generated and initiated a process. It is one thing to initiate and generate a development, and quite another to react and respond to it.[1] It is hardly necessary to add that reaction and response are not passive; they take place actively and generally by way of mobilization of a society's distinctive cultural resources. I need not pursue this theme here; it is the Weberian theme *par excellence*, the re-evaluation and re-examination of which is one of the most significant features of contemporary sociological discussion.

What then are the characteristics of 'Western' culture that may be deemed relevant to our present undertaking? Mention has already been made of the awareness of change and of the ways this awareness has become an object of analysis and a subject of interpretation, i.e., the self-interpretation and self-understanding of modern man. There is a great deal to be learned from Hegel also for our subject, as for so many other subjects. It is one

---

[1] In the terminology of other scholars, this distinction is one between 'endogenous' and 'imitative' development. The former is said by Lipset (1960, p. 94) to be more individualist and unconscious, the latter is described as post-revolutionary, deliberate and collective. On the same subject see also Gellner (1964, pp. 133–6).

thing to say, with Heraclitus or with orthodox Buddhism, that all things change and are impermanent, and quite another to be engaged in history in the manner of the modern West. Also in the sphere of religion, historical evolution is—to quote the words of W. C. Smith (1957)—'for the first time on a large scale becoming self-conscious . . . [it is] recognized, and in part deliberate'. Historicism may be poor, but for all I know we can't help being a kind of secular latter-day Franciscans, and as such should embrace the poverty of historicism as a Holy Poverty. But there is far more than historicism in Hegel. Hegel does not use the term 'secularization', yet he was, as Karl Löwith (Löwith 1950, 1952, 1971) has demonstrated, its great apostle and ideologist. He secularized the eschatological model of traditional Christianity by projecting the theological notion of *Heilsgeschichte* on to world history as such, and conversely raising world history to the level of a *Heilsgeschichte*. The fact that for Hegel the emancipation of bourgeois society was a stage in the process of the self-realization of the spirit, whereas for later generations emancipation came to mean total severance from the Christian moorings, is irrelevant for our present purpose, which is merely to illustrate how the reality meant by our terms 'secularity' and 'secularization' could be discussed even *avant la lettre*. Weber, too, makes only very sparing use of the word secularization, though he clearly deals with the subject. Of Tönnies it can be said that his *Gesellschaft* is a kind of secularized—one is almost tempted to call it a 'fallen'—*Gemeinschaft*, and his analysis is not devoid of the secularist's nostalgia. On the other hand we are all familiar with Roman Catholic usage according to which most parish priests are 'secular' clergy. Unlike the regulars and the 'religious', they can be 'laicized' but not secularized. But surely a secular priest is something very different from the self-appointed and self-ordained high priests of secularity, some of whom proclaim the 'death of God' with a fervour that exhibits all the symptoms of intense euphoria, and in a curious academico-theological liturgy celebrated in what has aptly been described as the pop-style of a 'happening'.

We may dispense here with an account of the fascinating history of the words secular, secularist, secularized, etc. For our purpose it suffices to note that, like other related terms, 'secularization' has more than one connotation and more than one function. There are at least three functions of the term that should be noted here. The word has served, and apparently still serves, not only as the scientific (or would-be scientific) designation of an historical-social, cultural as well as political process, but also as an ideological concept by means of which modern man attempts to interpret his historical and spiritual situation. It is thus one of our tools for constructing our historical reality, viz., our perception of it. As the German sociologists would put it, it is a *zeitgenössisches Interpretament*. This is tantamount to saying that it is even more than that: it is an ideological watchword and battle-cry in the struggle for the social construction of a cultural reality. In the words of H. Lübbe (1965), it is an *ideenpolitische* concept. Similarly David Martin (1969) accuses 'secularization' not only of suffering from the general poverty of historicism, but of projecting an ideological standpoint on our understanding of society. 'I do not regard secularization as involving a more or less unified syndrome of characteristics, subject to an irreversible master-trend. And I see the formulation of such master-trends as often rooted in ideological views of history.' It matters little, from this point of view, whether secularization is lamented as an unfortunate though inevitable fall from grace (i.e., from an allegedly more unified total religious culture), or hailed as a desirable and necessary progress. It is even possible, as we shall see later, to have the best of both worlds by celebrating secularization as the divine child of the very same Christian tradition of which it so radically emancipates itself.[1] In fact, one of the ideological functions of the theory of secularization seems to be the provision of theological ammunition for the claim that

---

[1] An unintended, and hence all the more amusing illustration is provided by the title of the English translation (*Protestantism and Progress*, 1912) of E. Troeltsch's *Die Bedeutung des Protestantismus für die Entstehung der Modernen Welt* (1911).

modernity is a religious, and more particularly a Christian, product. It is no wonder, therefore, that one of the most profound and thought-provoking discussions of the subject of modernity and secularization bears the title *Die Legitimität der Neuzeit* (Blumenberg 1966). The section in Blumenberg's book entitled *Säkularisierung—Kritik einer Kategorie geschichtlichen Unrechts* (pp. 9–74) should be required reading for all students of the subject. As regards the scientific use of the term, two connotations are relevant to our discussion. The one is secularization as the process of the emancipation of certain areas of social, cultural and political life from the dominance or control (be it only in the sense of ultimate legitimation) not only of ecclesiastical institutions but of traditional religious ideas and representations. The other is the implied allegation of continuity between certain ideas, values, orientations or structures in their present 'secular' form, and their religious antecedents, as happens quite frequently, e.g., when Marxism is described as a secularized form of biblical eschatology, or when peace, justice, the brotherhood of men or the 'sanctity of life' are advertised as secular versions of biblical ideals. There are a great many insufficiently explored assumptions behind these usages, e.g., the notion that earlier cultures were not only dominated in some sense (in which sense exactly?) by ecclesiastical institutions and authorities, but that they were also, in some other and not always clearly defined sense, more integrated and in their totality pervaded by 'religion'. Very often there is lurking in the background the oversimplified picture of an *idealtypische* total religious civilization—whether the Christian High Middle Ages in the West, or the age of the four rightly guided caliphs in Muslim traditional *mythistoire* or the Ashokan age for Buddhists. Even more important is the fact that whenever you say 'secular' you also, almost by definition, conjure up religion. Durkheim remarked that the only way to define the sacred was to say that it was the opposite of profane. Without going in for binary oppositions, we may nevertheless state that the use of terms such as secular, secularist, secularization of necessity implies a reference to religion.

These awkward and question-begging ambiguities have made some scholars wish to drop the term 'secular' altogether. Whilst sympathizing with their mood, I doubt the value of such drastic surgery as is proposed by, e.g., David Martin (1969): 'The word secularization should be erased from the sociological dictionary.' It would seem to me that precisely these ambiguities render the terminology so useful, in addition to presenting a challenge to our critical, analytical and methodological faculties. It is precisely the ambiguous position of the concept as both a watchword in the ideological struggles of Western civilization, and a scientific descriptive term which makes it so interesting and valuable. And whilst remaining constantly on the alert against hasty historicist derailment and illegitimate extrapolations from Western history, we should not rule out its possible usefulness also in the analysis of processes of modernization and of the crises of religion in non-Western societies.

The European, and in a wider sense Western, case also raises the problem of the relationship between secularization and modernity. When is secularization one of the contributing factors in the process of modernization (as was the case in Europe), and when is it the result or the concomitant of modernizing development? As with 'secularization' and 'secular', also 'modernization' and 'modern' are loaded terms hovering uneasily between ideological battle cry and analytical concept. Whatever the criteria and strategies which we employ to describe and measure that particular brand of cultural change called 'modernization', processes of secularization as well as of de-secularization (implying an earlier secularity) can be detected in it. The notion of modernity not only poses problems of method—Clifford Geertz (1968) has distinguished between the indexical, typological, world-acculturative and evolutionary—and of criteria (such as rationalization, viz. diffusion of secular-rational norms; degree of self-sustaining growth; increase in mobility; changes in the proportions of primary, secondary and tertiary occupations; urbanization etc.), it also smuggles into the discussion a certain normative dimension, e.g., when we describe certain contemporaries in our own culture, or certain other cultures, as psychologically, socially, economically, culturally or religiously 'not yet' modern, or as archaic, medieval, pre-modern or what-have-you.

Once again we find ourselves in the company of Max Weber, for what I have referred to just now as the smuggling in of a certain normative dimension, is not really very different from operating with ideal types—in this case the *Idealtyp* of modernity. But whereas the neo-Weberian sociologist will examine religions for their role in the process of modernization, our main emphasis will be on the question what modernization does to religion. The two questions cannot always be neatly separated, because it is precisely the Weberian approach—e.g., in the so-called Protestant Ethic theory—which stresses 'the existential and cultural foundations of any society committed to the mastery of this world through intensive discipline and consensual organiza-tion of the personal and social orders' (Nelson 1973). It is for this reason too that 'the proving grounds for Weber's views are not Prussia or even England, but the Soviet Union, the Far East, the Near East, Africa—in short, the world' (ibid.).

This salutary reminder by a sociologist may help us to evade, at least in part, the pitfalls of 'occidentocentrism' that I have mentioned before. I said that neither secularization nor moderniza-tion can be properly understood without taking into account their Western origins and the nature of the Western impact. Yet I would hesitate to echo Sir Hamilton Gibb's assertion—oversimplifying, as any good epigram is bound to be—'the truth of the matter is that modernization means "Westernization" ' (Gibb 1970). No doubt modernization occasionally meant a complete and total 'conversion to the West'—as in Kemalite Turkey, and conversely, the process of modernization in many non-Western societies was often rendered extremely complex precisely because of its Western origins and associations. As a result, processes of modernization were frequently affected by the intensity of anti-Western and anti-Christian animus present. More will be said on the subject in a subsequent chapter. But as a general rule, which applies to religion no less than to other dimensions of social and cultural reality, I would prefer to say, with Eisenstadt (1973b), that we must look in the various societies and cultures for 'the possibility of the development of parameters of modernity differing from the ones developed in Europe'. Modernization is not a trend of development defined by a uniform set of characteristics or indices, and irreversibly moving in a fixed direction. It should rather 'be seen as a process, or a series of processes with a common core generating similar problems, but to which different responses are possible'.

The spectrum of different responses includes a total, radical break with the past—at least on the manifest level—and the kind of 'cultural revolution' exemplified by, e.g., the Turkey of Mustafa Kemal (Yalman 1973) and, more recently, Mao's China, as well as diverse modes of integrating tradition, or elements from it, with the changes called modernity. Hence the enormous number of books and articles sporting in their titles such words as 'continuity and change', 'religion and change', 'tradition and modernization' or their synonyms in various permutations and combinations.

One thing, however, becomes fairly clear both from these titles and even more from the realities to which they are addressed. Modernity renders the past problematic. The past may cease to be the soil in which you have your roots and from which you draw life. At least you no longer do so in the matter-of-course manner of old. Instead, the past may become 'antiquated'. With special reference to religion, which is after all our subject, we may say that the 'fit' between the world we live in and life as we live it on the one hand, and the symbolic forms and institutions in which our forebears used to order it and make it meaningful has gone. What Peter Berger has called the 'plausibility structure' of established forms of faith and their symbolizations of reality and meaning has somehow become eroded or completely disintegrated. It certainly has lost its compelling quality. I cannot do better here than quote from Clifford Geertz (1968, pp. 3, 15):

established connections between particular varieties of faith and the cluster of images and institutions which have classically nourished them are for certain people in certain circumstances coming unstuck. In the new states as in the old, the intriguing question for the anthropologist is, 'How do men of religious sensibility react when the machinery of faith begins to wear out? What do they do when traditions falter?' . . .

They do, of course, all sorts of things. They lose their sensibility. Or they channel it into ideological fervor. Or they adopt an imported creed. Or they turn worriedly in upon themselves, or they cling even more intensely to the faltering traditions. Or they try to rework those traditions into more effective forms. Or they split themselves in half, living spiritually in the past and physically in the present. Or they try to express their religiousness in secular activities. And a few simply fail to notice their world is moving or, noticing, just collapse . . . Given the increasing diversification of individual experience, the dazzling multiformity of which is the hallmark of modern consciousness, the task of . . . any religious tradition to inform the faith of particular men and to be informed by it is becoming ever more difficult. A religion which would be catholic these days has an extraordinary variety of mentalities to be catholic about; and the question, can it do this and still remain a specific and persuasive force with a shape and identity of its own, has a steadily more problematical ring.

The crisis articulates itself in each religious tradition and in every society in different ways which we must seize in their distinctive individuality. But the general character of the religious dilemma has been well described by C. Geertz (ibid., p. 20) as

the internal confrontation of established forms of faith with altered conditions of life, and it is out of that confrontation that the resolution of that crisis, if there is to be a resolution, will have to come. If the term 'modernization' is to be given any substantial meaning and its spiritual implications uncovered, the connections between changes in the classical religious styles and such developments as rationalized forms of economic organization, the growth of political parties, labor unions, youth groups, and other voluntary associations, revised relations between the sexes, the appearance of mass communications, the emergence of new classes, and a whole host of other social novelties must be discovered.

At this juncture two other relevant considerations should be introduced, however briefly. The parent model, i.e., the Western form, of modernization has as one of its historical roots the criticism of religion. Not only modernity and secularization, but the very concept of secularization and secularity as handled in sociology and in the study of religions are rooted in the tradition of the enlightenment with its criticism of religion. This nexus, and the powerful tradition of the 'spirit of the enlightenment' together with its positivist and historicist offspring, place a heavy burden on the modern study of religion. The burden is not made lighter by the tendentiousness of the, at times, very thinly disguised so-called hermeneutical, phenomenological and other crypto-theological exercises in that field. Here I am repeating in slightly different words what I said before in connection with secularization. The modern study of religion is itself a 'secular' phenomenon. Hence when we study religion we not only try to understand a major historical and cultural phenomenon; we are—in the very act of doing so—already engaged willy-nilly in *Ideenpolitik*.

This leads me to the other point. When speaking of modernity many of us seem to refer not so much to something unheard-of new, but rather to a venerable tradition stretching from at least the Enlightenment to our own day. Modernity, as Professor M. Mahdi (1959) has so well put it, 'has itself become a tradition', although a peculiarly untraditional tradition. On the other hand there is the fact of what W. C. Smith (1957) has called the 'continuing newness of modernity for all mankind', and I suppose Professor Smith literally means *all* mankind and not only the 'as yet' pre-modern, traditional and developing societies. Elsewhere Professor Smith speaks of the apparently inherent 'instability of modernity'. But without wishing to minimize the utter and continuing 'newness of modernity', we must bear in mind that just as modernity, with all its openness and fluidity, has its own elements of tradition, so also tradition has its own plasticity and malleability. The very structure of both tradition and modernity is such that they cannot simply be reduced to a pair of opposites. As Edward Shils has pointed out with his customary insight and lucidity (Shils 1971, p. 122 f.), 'the mechanisms of persistence are not utterly distinct from the mechanisms of change. There is persistence in change and around change, and the mechanisms of change also call forth the operation of the mechanisms of persistence; without these, the innovation would fade and the previous condition would be restored.' Tradition means a certain 'presentness of the past', but this past is always being re-created and hence it 'is—to a significant extent—more than an "objective" past. It is also a past selectively re-created, re-shaped, re-set in a certain perception and in a context of relevance—for purposes of affirmation as well as of rejection by every generation . . .' This view of tradition can be generalized into the wider thesis (Gusfield 1973) that perception of a traditional culture is part of a group's self-identification. Members of a group simultaneously observe and discover their tradition as well as define it—thereby in some degree creating it. Their traditional culture is a belief and a statement about what is now perceived as having been typical in the past.

Hence we find that modernity has often been 'traditionalized' (Kothari 1968, pp. 273–93; 1970, p. 93) even as, by the same token, 'the traditional order is modernized . . . the stability of their relationship becoming itself an innovatory tradition' (Heesterman 1973b, p. 56). This creates a significant structural counterpoint, beyond tradition and modernity, to which we may have to return at a later stage after terminating our survey of contemporary religions. But enough has been said here to indicate why at least from the sociological point of view modernity is not by definition the pre-ordained grave-digger of tradition. 'Modernity is usually and implicitly credited with an irresistible power of impact. Perhaps the answer [why this is not quite so] can be found not in the much vaunted resilience of tradition as in the nature of modernity' (Heesterman 1973b, p. 35).

But if tradition changes by becoming modernized and modernity changes by becoming 'traditionalized', then one must take seriously into account the possibility that what used to be considered as modern until recently is already being overtaken by a newer modernity. In fact, sooner or later historians will have to make up their minds whether to use the term modernity as a movable indicator of temporal or cultural location, or as a fixed chronological term (as has happened, e.g., to the 'Middle Ages' which are no longer considered 'middle' by anybody, but serve as the designation of certain centuries). It is probably this type of awareness that has suggested to many the term 'post-modern' as being more adequate to the situation of at least some sections of (Western) humanity, and it is with this perspective in mind that I have ventured to call this series of lectures 'Beyond Tradition and Modernity', including the tradition of modernity. Whilst some religions are still on the road to modernity, modernity itself, with all its instability, is modernizing itself in a dialectical counterpoint to its own tradition. In fact, I had better admit that with my title I have simply been jumping on a fashionable post-modern bandwagon, namely the fashion of talking in 'Beyonds', as a mere glance at the catalogue of any religious library suffices to show: *Beyond Belief* (Bellah 1970), *Beyond Religion* (Jenkins 1962), the most recent contribution to the theology of Women's Lib entitled *Beyond God the Father* (Daly 1973), and many more. The last part of Milton Singer's excellent latest study of South India is entitled 'Beyond Tradition and Modernity in Madras'. Much of this 'Beyond' is, of course, typically Western and forms part of Western cultural history and more especially of an historicist *Epochenbewusstsein*, i.e., the awareness of standing between the twilight of a passing age and the possible dawn of a new one. Already a quarter of a century ago Romano Guardini wrote on *Das Ende der Neuzeit* (1950), and Eugen Rosenstock-Huessy spoke of 'overtaking modernity' (*Wir überholen die Moderne*). References to our 'post-Christian era' have become commonplace since the publication of Gabriel Vahanian's book in 1961. The theme will be taken up again in the next chapter. But since I promised to be unabashedly occidento-centric, permit me to conclude by explaining, somewhat crudely and by throwing out a few sample slogans, what I mean by post-modernity with special reference to religions. I shall not list and tabulate all the features that go into making up our post-modern scene, such as the decline of the West and the empowerment of hitherto powerless and/or subjugated societies; the Space Age of 'high-speed and fully-automated mechanical technologies, as well as of high-speed and fully-automated non-material information systems and microcircuitries' (Nelson 1973); the world of shrinking distance and quick transportation in which nevertheless thousands die of hunger every day. I shall rather stick as much as possible, for the sake of brevity, to names that can serve as slogans for cultural dimensions which I think are relevant to an understanding of present religious conscious-ness. My list of names suffers from being 'occidentocentric' as well as slanted to an intellectualist emphasis, but it must do for the moment even though we know that changes and shifts in religious consciousness and in the cultural and social locus of religion, are not a matter of the intellect only. Thus post-modernity means to me that the religious person is fully aware of living after Darwin, Marx, Freud, Weber and Durkheim. He is also aware of living after Kant, Hegel, Nietzsche, Dosto-yevski and Kierkegaard. If he is committed to a religious tradition that possesses Holy Scriptures, he also knows that he lives after Spinoza's *Tractatus* and after Wellhausen. He no longer wastes time on arguing with Wellhausen, or Freud, or Marx, or Darwin. Whatever his reservations regarding major or minor details, he takes them all for granted. And taking them for granted he asks: where do we go from here? What symbolic systems and frame-works of understanding are available that could set our personal lives, embedded as they are in social contexts and institutions, into a coherent pattern of meaning? Is the best that religions can perform in these circumstances a holding action, and the finding of ways and means to safeguard their heritage from what Gibb has called 'the corroding acids of our age'? If Gibb's phrase, originally used with reference to Islam, is deemed to be too pessimistic, then what is the role, if any, which specific traditions, that is to say the established forms of faith and the concomitant institutions of the great religious cultures, can play in creating, re-creating, salvaging, catalyzing or infusing universes of meaning that would somehow 'fit' the condition of man and society? Religion, in order to do any of this, would have to provide more than expressive outlets for emotions and for cosmic gut-responses. It would have to acquire a new plausibility that renders it not only intellectually acceptable and socially and individually meaningful, but also authoritative. Tradition has lost the authority that used to be inherent in it. Western religions claim that criticism of authority (and hence the resulting erosion of all authority) was as much part of their tradition as the sacralization of authority. Post-modern religion will not only have to discover its substantive contents, but also—and perhaps primarily—new canons of authority.

Virtue or Necessity: the Christian Encounter with Secularity

Vere dignum et iustum est, aequum et salutare—borrowing my prefatory words from the *praefatio* in the Roman mass—it is surely very meet and right, and perhaps even our bounden duty, to open our survey of religions in the modern age with a consideration of Christianity. The reasons for this priority should have become clear in the preceding chapter. We have seen that the problems and the types of change with which we are concerned here are products of Western culture. And Christianity is the religious dimension of this culture. No matter whether we view Christianity as the first victim of what is called modernity, or as its proud progenitor, or both, it is part of the same cultural matrix. The validity of this premise is not affected by the existence of non-Western forms of Christianity, or by the current efforts of Asian and African churches to de-Westernize themselves and evolve indigenous forms of Christianity. These latter developments are outside my present scope although they could serve as further welcome illustrations of the anthropological truism that also 'nativistic' movements and a renewed emphasis on the dimensions of indigenous cultures are 'revitalization' reactions to the impact and presence of the West. As regards our immediate subject, it is a comforting thought that for once, at least, the historical, sociological and theological vocabulary we use is legitimate, in spite of the unavoidable ambiguities which it entails and the confusion which it breeds. One may criticize the application to other cultures and religions of categories and concepts rooted in the particular history of the West; one cannot object to their use in the study of Western Christianity. But precisely because Christianity is the religious dimension of Western civilization, and modernization in non-Western societies is largely due to the impact of the West, it should occasion no surprise that Christian terminology at times also penetrates not only the study but even the self-expression of non-Western religions, much as Western literary and philosophical terminology penetrates the self-expression of non-Western cultures. (This is what I learned not so long ago when listening to a distinguished African intellectual explaining the nature of the black identity in terms of *négritude en-soi* and *négritude pour-soi*.) Let me repeat that this situation carries no implication of any inherent superiority of Christianity. It merely reminds us that Christianity is the religious dimension of Western culture and that it is therefore present, in one way or another, wherever Western influence, however indirect and oblique, is present.

As has been mentioned before, the term *saeculum* and its derivatives have had a long history, from antiquity to the seventeenth century. In the seventeenth century 'secularization' became a much used technical term, and we can trace its sub-sequent transition from the purely legal meaning of 'alienation of ecclesiastical property' to a designation of a process of cultural emancipation. This latter process in its turn must be understood in the context of Western intellectual history and more especially the history of the enlightenment. It may be useful to summarize once again some of the motifs, presuppositions and developments that form the background and stage setting of our subject, even at the risk of repeating some of the things that have already been said.

In the first place the very term secularization recalls to our mind an original dualism. This dualism can give rise to a variety of polarities, some of them within an overarching religious framework, others intending a radical disjunction. Thus surely Luther's doctrine of the state and of the 'two swords' is not an instance of modern secularization but a thoroughly theological conception. The distinction between 'religious' and 'secular' can be defined so as to make it very different from that between 'sacred' and 'profane', and both are different from the distinction between 'ecclesiastical' and 'secular'. But not only the original dualism can be expressed in a number of different variations; also each pole of this binary opposition lends itself to almost infinite differentiation. Thus, e.g., 'secular' and 'profane' need not be identical, and sociologists as well as theologians, each for their own reasons, propose increasingly subtle distinctions (e.g., secularization, profanization, de-sacralization, etc.). It then depends on the writer's ideological predilections which of these concepts (viz. cultural processes allegedly described by these concepts) receives a 'good' or a 'bad' rating. But whilst it could be argued that the dualism sacred-profane in one form or another underlies all religious phenomena, the pair religious-secular as current in our particular usage is a distinctly Western variation.

Secondly, we will recall that the peculiarly Western concept of secularization is not merely the product of the enlightenment in general, but of a very specific aspect of it: its criticism of religion. No doubt this criticism can also be welcomed as beneficial to religion. Many men of piety and faith have welcomed philosophical and scientific criticism of religion as a mechanism of theological purification, much as they welcomed the institutional extrication of religion from political or other mundane frameworks as a chance to cleanse religion from the corruptions of power. But every modern view of religion, even a positive and profoundly committed one, is heir to this enlightenment criticism and fully aware of its pedigree from the Deists to Hume, Voltaire, Kant, Hegel and Feuerbach and on to Marx, Weber, Durkheim and Freud. In its decisive eighteenth- and nineteenth-century stage this criticism articulated itself systematically by reference to Christianity. Old Testament Judaism and classical antiquity were referred to only incidentally and by way of occasional illustration. It is true that Judaism was not infrequently singled out for particularly hostile and scathing denigration, but this was due mainly to the fact that Judaism could conveniently serve as a vicarious whipping-boy at a time when direct and open attacks on the Church would have been too risky for their authors. Hegel's breadth of vision was exceptional, as was also the breadth of his actual knowledge of non-Western religions (Schoeps 1955), the high-handed arbitrariness of his interpretations notwithstanding. Yet his breadth of vision paradoxically

c

throws into relief his Christian occidentocentrism. Ancient Christian theologians would say that even pagan religions might be a providential *praeparatio evangelica*. Hegel, who surely did not intend to be a spokesman of either religion or the Christian faith, nevertheless came up with a refurbished version of the ancient doctrine by the manner in which he accorded to all religions a place in his construction of the development of the Spirit. For in his scheme or construction, Christianity functions not as one religion among others—not even as the highest—but as Absolute Religion, i.e., the quintessence of the concept of religion as such. Other liberal theologians, however much they might differ from Hegel in other respects, adopted his perspective. The great Harnack argued that Christianity was no positive religion like Islam or Judaism, but that it was 'religion as such'. Troeltsch, whose *Die Absolutheit des Christentums und die Religions-geschichte* sufficiently testifies to his concerns, considered Christianity to be not only the acme and climax of all religious development, but the point of convergence of all religious experience. In a way the modern theologians are doing exactly the same thing, only they do it by standing the traditional terminology on its head and affirming the superiority of Christianity on the grounds that it is not a religion. This, of course, is a theological mode of procedure, and theology is a normative science. We shall return in a later chapter to the fact that every religion of necessity possesses a *theologia religionum*, i.e., a system of classifying and evaluating 'other' religions as part of its efforts to define and interpret itself. Students of medieval Far Eastern Buddhism will be reminded here of the tradition of *kyō-han*. Even van der Leeuw's *Religion in Essence and Manifestation* which, as its subtitle indicates, was supposed to be a 'phenomenology of religion' always ends up, somewhat miraculously, with the structures of Christianity as the most highly developed, inclusive, or otherwise most meaningful. His phenomenology is, in fact, a theology in disguise.

I may seem to have deviated from my main subject, but the purpose of the deviation from Hegel to van der Leeuw was to show to what extent Western discourse on religion is determined by the Christian tradition. This holds true of enlightenment critics and *philosophes* no less than of theologians. Religion was perceived in terms of historical Christianity and its ecclesiastical structures, and attempts to arrive at a more generalized concept of religion were essentially generalizations on the basis of Christianity. Even the sociology of religion still bears this hereditary and apparently indelible trait, and one sympathizes with those scholars who maintain that, at least in the West, a serious sociology of religion is possible only as a sociology of Christianity. This programmatic statement is not, as might appear at first sight, an expression of a narrow parish-pump mentality but, on the contrary, of a sober recognition of the inherent limitations of our sociological traditions. What on earth can 'Church and Society' possibly mean in a Hindu context? The student of religion, if he really wants to avoid the limitations imposed by any one particular tradition, must opt for a comparative sociology and anthropology of cultures.

Enlightenment and post-enlightenment criticism has bequeathed to the modern world certain views and attitudes that have by now become almost axiomatic. Let me mention a random few: religions arise, develop and change in time and in response to specific historic and social situations; developments and changes are somehow related to the historical evolution of mankind (and this view in itself can generate religious philosophies, as illustrated by the case of Teilhard de Chardin); this evolution may reach a critical stage when scientific and social progress render many earlier religious institutions unacceptable and much of the symbolic—both conceptual and mythological —apparatus of religion obsolete. Religious institutions and representations are recognized to be products of human activity (even by theologians who then proceed to explain how they conceive the Divine to act through this human activity); they are projections of man, and as such can function properly only as long as their true projective character is unrecognized and remains unconscious. As we shall see in due course, modern apologists try to neutralize this challenge by admitting the essentially symbolic function of religion, but insisting that this function is expressive in a meaningful and legitimate way, rather than simply a compensation for man's weakness and inadequacy. Religion is, so to say, imaginative rather than imaginary. But even modern apologists will admit that one of the realities which religion so imaginatively expresses and re-creates is man's alienation. For all I know the theory of alienation may make a religious person much less uneasy than the praise which anthropologists and sociologists bestow on religion for its integrative functions. Any functionalist theory of religion ultimately comes down to the assertion that religion is not so much an opium as a placebo. For the definition of a placebo is that it works! But be that as it may, everyone will agree that religion undergoes a critical change and loses its innocence once we have 'exposed', as it were, its historical conditioning and psychological functions. I do not wish to be misunderstood. I do not advocate any form of reductionism as the inevitable consequence of eighteenth-, nineteenth-, or twentieth-century types of criticism. I merely suggest that religion loses its pristine, matter-of-course immediacy and 'innocence' once you begin to talk in historic terms of origins and development; in psycho-social terms of projection and alienation; in structural-functional terms of integration and —to cap it all—in terms of secularization when you want to conceptualize and interpret the nature of the change to modernity. No doubt there were heretics, atheists, materialists and plain cynics in matters of religion everywhere and at all times. A good many are known to the historians of religion, and many others are still waiting, entombed in libraries and MSS collections, to be resurrected by a Ph.D. student in quest of a subject for his dissertation. But we are not talking of individuals now but of dominant cultural styles and trends, and of major transformations in our collective, accepted 'plausibility structures'.

At this point it may be useful to remind ourselves again of two questions to which I have previously drawn attention. The one concerns the relationship of 'secularization' to other aspects of modernization. Much of course depends on how we define secularization. Weber, who rarely uses the term, clearly deals with the subject when speaking of the 'disenchantment of the world' and of rationalization. At any rate it should be clear that there are no unequivocal correlations between secularism or indifference to religion (by whatever indices we choose to measure these: ritual involvement, devotional practice, intellectual assent to theological propositions, religious knowledge or experience, motivations of conduct, etc.), and other facets of modernity such as urbanization, industrialization, mobility, occupational differentiation and so forth. You will have noticed, by the way, that I just said 'secularism *or* indifference to religion'. This was my way of indicating that it is possible to distinguish between secularism as an 'ism', that is as a *Weltanschauung*, and secularization as an historico-cultural process which may exhibit its own characteristic styles of religious commitment. Whilst I am not at all sure the distinction is really all that significant, it is nevertheless useful to know that it can be made. Our second question concerns the bearers of modernization, for clearly the mentality which we call 'modern' is not shared by all. Robert Bellah (1965) has spoken of the 'modernization of the soul'. The problem is of the first magnitude especially when studying societies in the course of development, for there the agents of modernization often are traditional, intellectual and/or bureaucratic elites. These modernizing elites are not necessarily secularist in the Western sense, and Nehru seems to have been exceptional rather than typical in that respect. In the Western world, however, it seems justified to view modernity, secularization, and the challenge of secularism to religion as interrelated aspects of one process, especially when the secularism of an elite is reproduced in a vulgarized form on other levels of society.

We now come to a crucial point in our argument. Whatever our various revised versions of the Weber thesis, there seems to be general agreement that the characteristic Western forms of modernization did not come out of the blue. Though not necessarily fruits of a purely Christian tree, they certainly grew on the soil of a culture whose attitudes, value orientations and motivational complex were shaped by Christianity no less than they shaped it. Whilst this genetic relationship is more or less taken for granted, there is even more emphatic assent, on the part of both historians and sociologists, to the proposition that the history of origins, interesting as it may be, is irrelevant to the nature of modernity. The boat of secular modernity has cut itself loose from its Christian moorings. It is precisely this essential autonomy, the fact that modernity cannot be derived from or exhaustively understood by reference to its genesis, and that it is (to use an expression coined by the philosopher Hartmann in another context) a *kategoriales Novum* which make modernity what it is.

It is also precisely the refusal to recognize this fact that highlights the ideological character of so much modern Christian theology. In fact, many of the most vocal theologians of secularity operate with a very distinct theory of history. They not only note the fact that Christianity can be instrumental in producing changes which then turn out to be inimical to it (cf. Edwards 1969) but they also celebrate this fact as evidence of the dialectical quality and hence implicit modernity of Christianity. They insist that secularization is a genuinely Christian achievement and the true fulfilment of the Christian *kerygma*. It can be traced back to Christ or possibly even to the Hebrew Bible where, as Weberians know, the process of 'disenchantment' first began. Curiously enough, this view of the pre-history of secularization is shared also by those who lament this fatal aberration of Western Christianity. Eastern orthodox thinkers like N. Berdiaeff (1945) who see themselves as carrying the banners of cosmic sacrament and mystery through the desert of our secularized age, would surely acquit the Bible or Jesus Christ of any complicity; the villain of the piece is *la pensée chrétienne occidentale*. Thomas Aquinas and Luther, and the traditions which they represent, have 'neutralized and secularized' an originally divine cosmos. But what is poison to a Berdiaeff is meat for the secular theologians in the West. With the parochial enthusiasm characteristic of revival preachers rather than of social scientists, they also proclaim that the secular achievement will of necessity spread, thereby proving the superiority of the Christian message (which, let us remember, is no religion!) over the religions of the world. The argument that the new theology is hardly compatible with what the New Testament says of Jesus Christ or what the Early Church taught will make little impression. The historian of religion will sympathize, for he knows, perhaps better than others, that attention to sound historical scholarship and a meticulous philological-exegetical discipline can seriously inhibit 'creative' theology. Students of the Hebrew Scriptures may raise their eyebrows at the way the New Testament (or the Talmud for that matter) handles the Old; this does not make the exercise less legitimate from the point of view of Christian (viz. rabbinic) theology. You do not read St Augustine on the Psalms in order to understand the Psalms; you do it in order to understand St Augustine. The same holds true of the modern theologians. Whether their message has anything to do with the Bible or with Jesus Christ is neither here nor there. What matters is that *they* think they have a message, and that they are sufficiently traditional and unmodern to feel compelled to articulate their message in Christological and biblical terms. The fact that in doing so they make light of historical and philological scholarship, and that their pneumatic exegesis is based on a modernized version of what used to be called homiletics but is now presented under the more impressive banner of 'hermeneutics', merely shows that in many ways they are less modern than they think. But then, if Heidegger is allowed to proffer his *midrash* on the pre-Socratics or Hölderlin, why should Paul van Buren, Harvey Cox and Dorothee Sölle not be permitted to do the same for the Bible or the 'Christ-event'?

The gospel of secularity, and the proclamation of the death of (the theistic) God as its extreme expression, have given rise to an enormous literature which exhibits considerable variety and should by no means be reduced to a simplifying common denominator. There are many excellent books on the subject, some purely descriptive and others also critical, so that I can dispense with an analysis of individual authors such as Vahanian, van Buren, A. van Leeuwen, Altizer, Hamilton, Robinson, Cox, D. Sölle—not to speak of the great father figures Bultmann, Tillich and Bonhoeffer. Likewise, we are not required here to join in the theological game of determining which writer is more 'dialectical'—one of the highest words of praise!—and which is more simple-minded. What needs emphasizing here is that many of these authors, in keeping with the spirit of the times, adopt a fashionable historical or sociological, often a Marxist jargon—existentialist language seems to be going out of fashion lately—and that they are doing so as apostles of a new *kerygma* and not in a serious sense as sociologists. In fact, their sociology is often very dubious, and examples of combined theological and sociological reflection of a high order (as, e.g., in the work of Trutz Rendtorff in Germany) are few and far between. David Martin (1969) has poked some gentle fun at the theologians playing sociologists and at the discomfiture of the professional sociologist 'fallen among theologians', and I need say no more on the subject. This means that we have to discuss the secular theologians, and discuss them seriously, for what they are: not analysts of a given situation but symptoms of it, and very *engagé* apostles of a new *kerygma*. Considering the passionate and euphoric fervour with which they proclaim their message, they might well be called the hot-gospellers of a new religious revival. Their preaching is also characterized by a typical revolutionary syndrome: the assurance of being in the vanguard—like every revolutionary elite—of the new consciousness with which the *profanum vulgus* have not yet caught up. There is a kind of theological one-upmanship involved here: whose theology is more modern, more revolutionary, and more radical—the latter being the highest praise that can be bestowed. Professor W. C. Smith (1967) has commented on the old-fashioned, dogmatic self-righteousness of the new theology which, with traditional exclusiveness, advertises its views as the only valid interpretation of Christianity. Obviously the death-of-God theologians want to say that other people's ideas of God are wrong (Smith, p. 31). Smith correctly detects the classical missionary's cultural and theological aggressiveness against the rest of the world behind much of this enthusiastic evangelism. There is, in fact, a curious incongruence between the revolutionary and radical façade, and the apologetic intention behind it. A sophisticated apologetic no doubt, but apologetic nonetheless. Surely modern secular man does not require a refurbished theology in order to realize his freedom, his commitment to his fellow-man, his social and political responsibility, and so on and so forth. An existentialist can without difficulty share Bultmann's interpretation of the human situation without feeling the least need of a kerygmatic *evangelium secundum Bultmann* as a peg on which to hang his existential awareness. Paul van Buren will no doubt agree that some people might experience the call to freedom by meditating on Socrates rather than on Christ. And many religious people who draw strength from their traditional liturgies may be profoundly aware of the implications of their faith for political and social action without resorting to what must appear to them as the rigmarole of a *politisches Nachtgebet*. In one respect at least the new theologians are therefore not a bit more modern than their colleagues in the non-Western religions. We shall see in subsequent chapters how religions can function as vehicles of modernization by allowing their scriptures and other symbols to serve as coding devices. Thus Muslim modernists find their contemporary values in the Qur'an; and not only Shankara and Ramanuja but also Tilak, Aurobindo and Gandhi expressed their views by writing commentaries on the Bhagavad Gita or invoking its authority. Harvey Cox produces Christian warrant first for his encomium to the Secular City (1966) and the optimism of the New Frontier, then (Cox 1969) for his defence of hippie ethic, and more recently (Cox 1973) for his apology for the new forms of self-fulfilment and turning inward prevalent among certain sections of the American public and more especially among former political activists. In the circumstances it is inevitable that there are some who feel that the much advertised

secular and radical theologies of our day simply pander to anything that appears to be liberated or 'in', and that they are
clever, though anything but convincing exercises in jumping on
the bandwagons of the *Zeitgeist*. The market—clearly obeying the
laws of demand and supply—is flooded with one 'in' theology
after the other: theologies of liberation, of revolution, of hope,
of play, of ecology, of Women's Lib, political theology, black
theology, not to speak of theologies after-the-death-of-God. Of
course it is only natural for religions, and Christianity is no
exception, to try and demonstrate their 'relevance' to whatever
'present circumstances' humanity finds itself in. This ardent quest
for relevance may find (literary) expression in such titles as *The
Church Serves the Changing City* (Sanderson 1955) or *God and the
H-Bomb* (Keys 1961). Something will be said later about the
charge that much current theology is an elaborate exercise in
making a virtue of necessity. But there is a difference between a
realistic quest for relevance and the frenzied race to be with the
'in' thing. One critic has described Harvey Cox (and he is
representative of a certain style in contemporary religious
writing) as 'a public relations official of the *Zeitgeist*, department
of religious affairs' (Mintz 1974). And in a less journalistic style,
a serious sociological analysis (Nijk 1968) concludes that
'contemporary [theological] thinking on secularization is, in
fact, an attempt to salvage at any price some kind of "definition
of reality" from the bankruptcy estate of what used to be the old
accepted Christian truths'.

There is some truth in all these judgments, though the historian of religion should try, as he is in private duty bound, to
be less sarcastic, more understanding and, if possible, even a
little more charitable. It is not the dubious intellectual quality
or the questionable consistency of the new theology which concerns him in the first place, not even the rhetorical flourishes
obfuscating the distinction between the death of God as an
allegedly objective 'event' (whatever that means), and the death
of the idea of God, viz. of man's belief in God (which is conceiv-
able even if God is held to have never existed). We are concerned

here with the new theology as a profound religious concern struggling for expression. As has been said before, we are dealing with a religious revival. It is a religious revival of unique interest to the student of religion, because it is religious and at the same time wants to face up to the challenge and reality of atheism.

Leaving aside the more vulgar forms of atheism, we may say that Christianity (as also some other religions) has always had a tradition of taking what appeared on the surface to be atheist-type criticism seriously. The medieval *theologia negativa* is one instance. The late Melkite Patriarch Maximos IV Sayyegh is reported to have said, with his usual forthrightness, 'the God the atheists don't believe in is a God I don't believe in either'. Matters are, in reality, not quite that simple, especially as modern atheism since Nietzsche has cast itself in a heroic role: atheism is heroism, whereas religion allegedly seeks easy consolations. The heroic stance, too (Sartre is among its latter-day representatives), is an oversimplification, but Christian theologians have taken the challenge of atheism seriously even when they were convinced, both in faith and in reason, of its inadequacies. One thinks—to give but a few random examples—of H. de Lubac's *Le drame de l'humanisme athée* (1959), Jean Lacroix, *Le sens de l'athéisme moderne* (1958, published with ecclesiastical *imprimatur*), Michael Novak's *Belief and Unbelief* (1965), or Thomas Merton's review of Bishop Robinson's *Honest to God* in *The Commonweal*, lxxx, no. 19 (21 August 1964). The new radical theologians, however, want to take atheism even more seriously—with a 'deadly' serious-ness that goes to the very limits of what seems to them to be secular modernity, and there plunges into the baptismal font of a new religious experience. It is the subjective testimony to this experience that is of interest to the student of religion, even if he cannot take the accompanying, intellectually poor but all the more arrogant, theological lucubrations very seriously. The radical theologians have been described by one perceptive observer (Hartmann 1969) as a kind of modern counter-pietists. Whereas the old pietists identified their subjective experience of the presence of God with his objective presence, the radical theologian identifies his subjective experience of a passing away of God with an objective, historico-metaphysical event. But for a Christian, unlike a Theravada Buddhist (though Buddhists also can be too glib in talking about atheism), the experience of atheism is a very serious, indeed shattering matter which goes far beyond anything that can be handled with the tools of the venerable *theologia negativa* or even of Paul Tillich. In order to articulate his new religious sensibility and confirm his own sense of 'modernity', the new and radical theologian feels impelled to symbolic acts—and for a theologian this means verbal symbolism. One of these symbolic acts is the solemn rejection of earlier symbols, in this case of the symbolic nouns 'God' and 'religion'. Since most ordinary people appear to be perfectly capable of committing themselves to social and political responsibility and action even without the weird ideological apparatus of the new theology, one must see the latter as a 'rebound' phenomenon. The 'rebound' is due to a very Christian disappointment with the historical record of the Visible Church. To the modern mind the image of the Church is that of a force of oppression rather than liberation, of stagnation rather than progress, and of a total failure to come anywhere near to living up to its verbal commitments to social change (cf. Houtart and Rousseau 1972). It is not so much with such reactionary documents as *Rerum Novarum* in the last century, and *Humani Generis* not so very long ago in ours that Christians have trouble—these pronunciamentos are already too obsolete to claim the attention of any but professional antiquarians. The difficulty is rather with the allegedly more up-to-date statements produced by Vatican II which, far from blazing new trails, merely try to catch up—not without audible gasping and panting—with the moral imperatives and sensibilities of a secularized world. In the circumstances the claim that the Church today has a 'prophetic mission' to the world has a somewhat hollow ring, in spite of the frenetic involvement of some church groups and organizations in 'politics of liberation' and the like. The shrinkage of much traditional 'explicit religion' to limited areas of the 'sacred' (i.e., in the main, to dogma and ritual) accounts for the new gospel of shrinkage in the direction of secular-activity-in-the-world. Flushed with the euphoria of discovery—the discovery of new areas of legitimate religious activity—the new theologians are merciless in their exposure of the poverty of traditional religion. They must be excused for not yet having had time to discover the poverty of their own gospel.

Having persistently referred to the new theology as a religious revival, a short apology is in order here, especially with a view to the claim of the former to preach a religionless Christianity. My apology may have the additional advantage of illustrating once more the differences of approach of theologian and historian of religion. The modern watchword has an interesting history, and it surely is significant that in our century 'religion' should have become almost a dirty word, not with atheists, materialists (dialectical or otherwise) and similar unbelievers, but with a certain brand of theologians. Thus a certain type of Protestant neo-orthodoxy eagerly embraced whatever made a good, old-fashioned believer shudder. Everything was grist to the theologian's mill: biblical criticism, sociology, psychology—provided it helped to show up religion for what it is: the human, all-too-human opium of fallen man, constructing for himself, at times in the most devious ways and by the most sophisticated methods, elaborate systems for comforting himself, deceiving himself, or otherwise trying to evade *la condition humaine*. Religion is, in fact, the supreme attempt of man to evade the problem of his existence; it is the triumph of human autonomy even when it disguises itself as dependence on the very gods which it has created, and hence it is ultimately the worst of sins. The only real way of salvation is therefore not 'religion'—for religion is a bad thing; something which the others, those poor misguided fellows, have—but the action of God, the judgment of God and the grace of God. It would be unfair to attribute this attitude exclusively to Protestant neo-orthodoxy and Karl Barth. I can think of Jewish (Professor I. Leibovitz) and Muslim (A. Mahdoodi) counterparts, where, of course the central saving category, i.e., that which saves man from his anthropocentric autonomy and all its works and projections, is not faith but obedience to a God-given law. What all these have in common is the horror of human autonomy as their basic anthropological stance. Salvation comes from heteronomy—an understandable reaction to the neo-Kantian period of liberal theology. Now, of course, there is no reason at all why the unregenerate outsider, lacking the necessary grace, should not view these theological lucubrations as just one more example of, *horribile dictu*, religion; one more pathetic, devious and rather naïve attempt to provide an answer to man's anguish. Even the rejection of 'religion', the radical criticism, the prophetic judgment on all human efforts, the both humble and arrogant flight to redeeming heteronomy may well be interpreted as a thoroughly human reaction—by way of projection—to the human predicament since, as we all know, self-transcendence is one of the essential characteristics of human nature. Indeed, it is *the* human function *par excellence*.

The modern theologies of secularity are, as has been said before, evidently on the rebound, and represent a reaction against the Barthian disengagement of the gospel from culture and society, whilst retaining the Barthian rejection of religion. For to reject Barth does not necessarily mean to go back to Schleiermacher. You can instead go one better and produce a more contemporary version of the idea that Christianity is not religion: a theology after the death of God, the mythology of an existential or *engagé* Christ taking the place of a defunct, pre-modern mythological God, and an anti-institutional gospel that can be realized only through involvement in culture and social relations. For our purposes the modern faddist distinction between religion (which is bad) and the one true religion which is, by definition, no religion at all, can be dismissed. Let us instead praise, or at least understand, the most recent revival in the history of Western Christianity. Like every articulate religious expression, it uses not concepts but symbols. Symbols are easily confused with concepts when the two are homonymous. In any case there is much two-way traffic from the one to the other. Symbols, even mythical ones, can become concepts, and concepts can become re-mythologized (as happened, e.g., in Gnosticism). Such double-faced symbol-*cum*-concept nouns can be found everywhere: truth, freedom, *prajnaparamita* are such words. The word 'God' is more a symbol than a concept. The 'death of God' is a pure symbol. Some key words have been used before in a less strident and programmatic fashion, e.g., man's 'coming of age' by Kant, and the death of God by Hegel. But today these words have acquired a new symbolic resonance and function—not only the 'death of God' and *Mündigkeit*, but also 'modern', 'secular', 'radical', 'revolutionary', 'biblical'. Some of these symbols have a positive rating (e.g., 'freedom' or 'secularity'), others a negative one (e.g., 'religion'). Hence Daniel Jenkins (1962) was right when describing religionless Christianity as a catchphrase used 'more to indicate an awareness . . . than to define something which is clearly formulated'. Whether these symbols are solid and intellectually substantial enough to remain meaningful and to communicate a more permanent sense of validity, or whether they merely have an immediate exclamatory letting-off-steam sort of function only the future will show.

The times seem to have passed when religions precipitated, released or channeled new spiritual and social dynamisms. Perhaps Methodism in England was one of the last instances, in the West, of a genuinely religious movement shaping and transforming the moral climate of a society. Today religions can at best hope to respond to challenges and to make some sense of, and discover some meaning in, the realities in which they find themselves. The new theology is a response of religion like any other. It is unique in that it is a Western Christian response to a uniquely Western situation. Some of the elements characterizing this situation have been mentioned before: secularization, modernization, rationality, loss of traditional frameworks of meaning and symbolic reference. Loss also of the sense of meaningfulness of the traditional articulation of the Christian community, i.e., the Church. The response to this loss is typically Western not only in its substance, but also in its styles:

pop-style, hippie-style, revolutionary style. These styles, too, have their function in the economy of salvation. At best they are harbingers of something new, at worst they are legitimate protests against a past which does not manage to bury its dead. Whilst some enthusiasts solemnly celebrate the revolutionary radicalism of their theology, others, even more to the left, will denounce this allegedly revolutionary and secular theology as just another example of 'false consciousness' and of an extremely well-disguised bourgeois ideology. *Et le jeu continue.*

Do these theological trends usher in the end of Christianity, predicted by some observers also on other grounds (e.g., statistical and sociological findings)? Historians of religion should wear the academic's gown and not the prophet's mantle, but they have learned something about the resilience of religions and about the dialectics of continuity and change in the symbolic configurations of the great traditions. Even more to the point, they have learned something about the nature and structure of both tradition and modernity (see above, pp. 16-17). All religions have passed through major transformations. Some heresies have remained heresies, others have become orthodoxies. There were fundamentalist Jewish zealots who wished to excommunicate the great twelfth-century philosopher-theologian Maimonides for his radical denial of all anthropomorphisms, including all positive attributes of God. A few centuries later the rabbis were ready to excommunicate anyone who held that the biblical anthropomorphisms were originally meant to be taken literally. The heresies of Copernicus, Darwin and Wellhausen are gratefully accepted by later generations of believers, not only because they represent scientific truth but because—as scientific truth—they help to purify religion from false assumptions and elements, and force it to define itself in more adequate ways.

The mechanisms of change and adaptation vary, though one may feel tempted to subsume them under the heading 'how to make virtues of necessities'. Fortunately there are temptations that should not be resisted, and this seems to be one of them. Is not all of life an adaptation to, and a coping with, necessities?

Is it not meet and proper that the realities and imperatives of life should be considered, in the human perspective, as necessities of which we should make virtues? And—to conclude with a final rhetorical question—is it not the case that men of faith have always known and testified that the world's and man's necessity *par excellence* was God or, more precisely, that which is symbolized by this word or its equivalents? If they were right, then there can be no greater virtue than responding to this necessity.

Sacral Particularity: the Jewish Case
(with a digression on Japan)

From the point of view of the Comparative Religionist, Judaism occupies a disconcerting half-way house in more than one respect. There is, to begin with, its interesting position between the universal and the particular, as will become clear from the following fairy-tale.

Once upon a time all religions were particularistic. Like languages or other social phenomena and institutions, they had their natural growth in natural communities—whether tribes, cities, or states—and they were essentially concerned with the needs of the group also in its dealings with the supernaturals— the ancestors, the gods, or god. Even the ancient Israelites, although they knew that 'all the gods of the nations are but godlings, and the Lord has made the heavens' and although their descendants repeat thrice daily in their prayers 'for they [*scil.* the nations] bow down to vanity and nothingness, and pray to a god that cannot help', would nonetheless express their fidelity to their God Yahweh in these terms: 'For all people will walk every one in the name of his god, and we will walk in the name of Yahweh our God for ever and ever' (Micah 4: 5). Biblical and post-biblical Israel did not, as a rule, desire or attempt to impose its worship on others. Yet its breakthrough to universalism implied a certain degree of exclusiveness, intolerance and, indeed, fundamental negation of other religious traditions. It was no longer merely a question of letting every people legitimately serve its gods, but of insisting at the same time that these gods were vanity and nothingness. Whilst most ancient and primitive religions were ethnocentric and hence tolerant—for other religions have the same right to exist as other peoples; in fact, they are one dimension of the existence of these other peoples— Israelite religion admitted the permissibility of other religions for others, but emphatically denied their truth and their reality-value. This is, no doubt, a poor kind of tolerance, since it is not material but at best purely formal as regards outside groups. It allows for co-existence, but excludes communion with others.

The religions that came in the wake of Judaism claimed universality in an even more far-reaching sense, and hence their universalism, that is to say their intolerance, was both internal and external, material and formal, intensive and extensive. Universalist religions have taken considerable pride in their universalism, vaunting it as a major virtue and looking down with a certain contempt on, e.g., Judaism and its narrow-minded and ethnocentric particularism. They rarely rendered account to themselves of the 'centrism' of their own attitudes, and of their fundamental unwillingness to accept, let alone respect or appreciate, the specific individuality and integrity of other religious groups. It matters little for our present purpose whether this universalist intolerance is practical or merely theoretical, whether it expresses itself in aggressive or otherwise offensive missionary activity, in less militant 'testimony', or in purely doctrinal positions. The fact remains that the classical Christian missionary is not the right man to help you understand Islam or Hinduism. One shudders to imagine what the rhapsodically universalist prophet known as the Second Isaiah would have had to say to someone desirous of a deeper appreciation of say ancient Babylonian or Greek religion. But then the universalistically minded are having an easy time: they mostly define their problem in terms of the relationship between the great universal religions of today, and they rarely bother about the primitive and 'dead' religions which they gladly leave to the anthropologists and to the historians respectively.

The truth of the matter is that the nature and moral quality of both 'universalism' and 'particularism' are less unequivocal than is often assumed. Universalism is often expansionist precisely because it is universalist also in its determination to suffer no other gods; it is, indeed, universalistically exclusive. Particularism, on the other hand, having no universalist pretensions, may appear to admit of co-existence and even to harbour possibilities of a pluralistic respect for the individuality and integrity of other religious configurations. Ethnocentrism and intolerance are not necessarily related. In fact, it could be argued that they are related in inverse ratio.

To put the same thing in different words: particularism (as an 'ism') is different from the affirmation of particularity. Universalism is very often little more than a euphemistic name for the imperialist-expansionist pretensions of a particular religion or ideology. A genuine human universality, it could be argued, is made up of particularities. The human community is not necessarily a community of individuals—that artificial construct of rationalist minds—but a community of communities. This much seems fairly evident today, when pluralism is being widely affirmed as the one acceptable basis of universality. The student of religion will note in passing that—as Peter Berger has shown—there is a close connection between pluralism and secularization. As applied to our present subject this means that Judaism, with all its temptations of ethnocentrism and exclusiveness, also harbours a potential paradigm for a meaningful variation on the theme of the dialectic between particularity and universality.

Secondly, Judaism comes closest to Christianity in its involvement in modernity and secularity. This is due to the fact—or to the historical accident, if you prefer—of the emancipation of Western Jewry. The history of this emancipation is rooted in the European enlightenment and its growing ideals of tolerance. European Jewry did not enter modern European society in a long process of 'endogenous' gestation and growth, but they plunged into it as the ghetto walls were being breached, with a bang, though not without prolonged whimpers. Moreover the Jews were not merely the beneficiaries of modernity and secularization but also among their most active and dynamic agents—not of their genesis, to be sure, but in the development of these processes. Their intellectual capacities, their moral and social sensibilities, their desire for social mobility and advancement as well as their messianic ardour all poured into a secularizing modern

European civilization and contributed to its development in all spheres: economic, scientific, academic, artistic, socialist and revolutionary. Small wonder that the conservative and nostalgic defenders of the idea of an integral European-Christian civilization felt unhappy and saw the Jew as an agent of disintegration and subversion. Very similarly also the conservative leadership in the ghettos, far from welcoming emancipation, dreaded what they felt to be a threat to traditional faith and order. In our more modern language: they sensed the danger of an erosion of Jewish substance and identity. The conservatives in both camps, each for his own reasons, preferred a less open society. For the Jew the ghetto or *millet* was preferable to loss of identity through secularization and assimilation; the Christian did not want his culture to be adulterated by the influx of alien elements.

The population should be homogeneous ... Where two or more cultures exist in the same place, they are likely either to be fiercely self-conscious or both to become adulterate. What is still more important is unity of religious background ...

You may think that these two sentences were written by a very reactionary Zionist ideologist, but I have to disabuse you on this point. The quotation does not refer to Israel, and is taken from T. S. Eliot, who concludes, in the same paragraph, that 'reasons of race and religion combine to make any large number of freethinking Jews undesirable'. Please note the 'freethinking Jews'. They alone are apt to act as a leaven or yeast, penetrating, transforming and secularizing (which to some people is tantamount to disintegrating) a previously homogeneous Christian society, whereas the orthodox or at least the denominationally committed Jew may carry enough of the ghetto within and about himself to be *in* the surrounding society but not *of* it. This is ultimately the traditional *millet* formula—a formula that seeks to safeguard co-existence but to prevent communion.

Even where emancipation did not lead to total assimilation—anti-Semitism from outside and the strength of the Jewish resources from within could often prevent it—it certainly could not ward off the danger of spiritual, psychological and social alienation of which certain forms of Jewish self-hatred were among the most tragic manifestations. This was true especially in the European setting where emancipation often had to be bought at the price of assimilation to the politico-cultural entity of the *Nationalstaat*. It was different in America with its pattern of denominational pluralism. The national—social as well as cultural—revival known as Zionism attempted to give its own answer to what were felt to be the two equally undesirable alternatives of the ghetto on the one hand, and of a not only incomplete and unsuccessful but also ambiguous and alienating emancipation on the other. It is one of the ironies of history that the Jews, who in certain situations welcomed the secularist, open society, would echo in other circumstances the views quoted above from T. S. Eliot, in the interest of preserving their historical identity and character. Diaspora Jewry thrives on the separation of Church and State and is, in a way, intent on de-Christianizing the Christian nations, just as Arab Christians are intent, in the interests of their own survival, to de-Islamize and to secularize Arab nationalism. At the same time the Jews also realize that they have returned to Palestine not merely to establish one more pluralist utopia, a *polis* of rational beings, or an asylum for the persecuted, but in order to achieve a fullness of Jewish life and to fulfil a Jewish destiny. In the present state of the world, this seemed to them to imply the necessity of a 'Jewish State'. The return to the ancient land makes sense, in Zionist ideology, only as a corporate effort to create a new Jewish life—not as a denomination but as a body politic. Hence all public buildings in Israel have a *mezuzah* at their doors and Jews appear to be heartily glad of it—not because they all affirm the theological implications of a *mezuzah* but because, like national colours or a coat of arms, it demonstrates Jewish identity. Needless to say that the same Jews would be very much upset if the City of New York declared itself so Christian as to require that a crucifix be put up in every room in every public building. Yet for all its being a nativistic revitalization movement (if I may borrow from our current anthropological jargon), Zionism also bore the marks of modern Western culture: its secularism, its modernity, its socialism and its nationalism. This, incidentally, also creates serious dichotomies inside Jewry. I referred in a previous chapter to the problem of identifying the bearers of modernity. As far as Judaism is concerned, it is Western Jewry which since the emancipation is 'modern'. Even the orthodox are modern on the economic and on several social and cultural levels. The secularists are modern also on further cultural and intellectual levels. Conservative and Reform Judaism try to be modern also on the religious and theological levels. This situation is in evident opposition to that of oriental Jewry who are in many ways pre-modern, and it constitutes a major source of tension also in the State of Israel. Hence 'modern' Jewish thinkers may be unable to communicate not only with their more orthodox brethren of western provenance, but also with those sections of the Jewish community that are being plunged into a modern setting without sharing the cultural dimensions and presuppositions of the latter.

However, before pursuing this line further, let us remind ourselves that Judaism is also a religion. If I may anticipate the terminology to be used in a later chapter, it is not merely *jinsīyah* but a *dīn allah*. In its specifically religious (or perhaps I should be more precise and say in its theological) aspects, Judaism today is heir to all the problems and difficulties besetting religions in general and theistic religions in particular. The major symbols and concepts in which Jewish religious consciousness has articulated itself and around which it has crystallized, have become problematic: God, creation, revelation (and more especially the notion of a Sinaitic revelation and of *Torah* as the uniquely authoritative repository of this revelation), the meaning of redemption, and many more. I purposely do not discuss those elements in the Jewish tradition that can easily be de-mythologized or allegorized away. Jewish theology has a long history of re-interpretation, allegorization, and de-mythologization as well as re-mythologization. I am speaking here of what are generally considered fundamentals. Thus it matters little that in many expressions of Jewish thought the emphasis has shifted from a personal messiah to messianic redemption and a messianic order. (Hence, by the way, also the utter irrelevance, for a Jewish-Christian dialogue, of the Christological issue—at least in some of its simplistic formulations). What does matter is the question how Judaism today envisages 'redemption' as a central *religious* category. What does it mean to speak of God at a time when even those who do not proclaim his death admit his absence or eclipse? And what exactly does it mean, in the light of the experience and sensibilities of modern man, to speak of a 'God or History'? I do not refer here specifically to the Jewish experience of the Holocaust, a subject still too overwhelmingly close in its stark horror to admit of academic discussion. I would insist, however, in passing, that any theological or anti-theological conclusions drawn from the Holocaust are not determined by the character of Auschwitz, but by the modern mind that responds to it. R. L. Rubenstein's *After Auschwitz* (1966) has been hailed by William Hamilton as the Jewish contribution to the death-of-God movement. Rubinstein perhaps did not reflect that for many centuries those of his ancestors who survived pogroms and massacres would compose more prayers and liturgies, and institute new fasts rather than despair of God. Moreover, something seems to be fundamentally wrong with, or at least distinctly unpalatable about, the ethnocentrism of a Jewish theology that takes the Huns, Djengis Khan and the genocide of the Armenians in its stride, but suddenly balks at Auschwitz. In other words, it is in the modern mind's reaction and not in the event as such that the crisis is located. And as we move from academic theology to the realities of history we find that the response to Auschwitz was more intense loyalty, stronger commitment, and even the re-establishment of a Jewish commonwealth, the State of Israel.

But let us return to the theological questions with which we began. The account of creation in Genesis 1–2, especially when it is not taken literally, challenges the modern believer with even greater urgency to face up to the problem of creation as such, i.e., the problem of the apparently self-explanatory and self-sufficient character of the cosmos and the fullness thereof, and of its relation to that transcendence of which faith speaks. What does a Jew mean by revelation—at least if he wants to take the term seriously and not metaphorically, and more especially if it signifies not an incarnational-kerygmatic event but an event of a different order: the giving of the Torah? It is surely unnecessary to insist once again that the student of religion, unlike the theologian, cannot pronounce on the 'revealed' character of any religion. All he can do is to distinguish, in Usener's terms, between *Offenbarungsreligion* and *geoffenbarte Religion*, i.e., between revelation-type of religion and revealed religion. On the latter he has nothing to say. The former is neither a theological nor a metaphysical, but a descriptive and typological term. Its purpose is to distinguish between religions which claim a revelation as their source, and systems which do not make this claim. If we examine religious claims about revelations we find that precisely as there is no natural religion but only specific, positive religions, so there is no such thing as a general revelation but only individual revelations or, to be more exact, individual experiences or traditions of revelation. Revelation as an abstraction without phenomenal content is meaningless. Revelation as the self-revelation of God or of transcendence to somebody is thus structurally different from other experiences of sudden insight or deepened awareness which are perhaps better described as illuminations, intuitions and the like. Since revelation is an empirical term describing a definite experience or tradition, the assertion that 'history' or 'nature' are the media of a general revelation can only mean that they are potential *loci* of specific revelation-experiences, precisely because they have functioned as such in the past. And once we are determined to dignify certain phenomena with the prestige-word 'revelation', why not apply it to anything we think to be good, or beautiful, or noble, or challenging? Why not apply it also to a Beethoven String Quartet, or a Bach fugue, or—lest my musical tastes seem to be too square—to Rock n' Roll, especially as some years ago I learned from a progressive sheet which I picked up on the campus of Columbia University that 'rock music points an accusing finger at society for the state the world is in. It speaks of a new order. A world where people are real and values are just'. Clearly rock music has taken over the functions of Amos and Isaiah. Let us hope with better success.

Many spokesmen of Reform Judaism seem to have suffered from a similar delusion. They, too, seem to have believed that muddled thinking could make good theology and hence they talked much about 'progressive revelation'. But why revelation? And who is it that reveals himself? Why not progressive evolution, or progressive discovery, or progressive awareness? And if it be said that one man's revelation is another man's discovery, then let us at least respect the specificity of the various experiences and not force them into the mould of our pet theological jargons.

For Jewish orthodoxy the problem of revelation and Torah is compounded by the need of legitimizing the continued authority of the *halakhah*. This leads to a peculiar kind of Jewish fundamentalism and to such odd results as the rejection, to this day, by the orthodox of Biblical ('Higher') Criticism, at least with regard to the Pentateuch. It is said of one very respectable institution of rabbinic learning that the Pentateuch is not taught there at all, because ignoring Higher Criticism would be incompatible with scholarly integrity whilst taking it into account would compromise the faith.

At this juncture we must revert again to a characteristic feature of Judaism which has been briefly mentioned before. I am using the term 'Judaism' here as a kind of shorthand for the 'Religion of Israel' or 'Religion of the Jewish People'. In other words, we are dealing here with a religion that has a people as its bearer and which cannot be divorced—at least not without violence to the facts—from its ethnic, communal and socio-civilizational dimensions. This quality of Judaism has to be emphasized especially at a time when it is often suggested, openly or surreptitiously, that a religion has to be universal in order to be

respectable. Even so, to describe Judaism as the religion of the
Jewish people is already slightly misrepresenting the situation.
Judaism is the religious dimension of the Jewish people. Israel—
to call the people by the name by which since biblical times they
called themselves—is a people born of, and with, religion. I am,
of course, not trying to reconstruct the stages of the undoubtedly
very complex early historical developments, but rather attempting
to formulate what has been the Jews' understanding of themselves and their historical existence. No matter how and when
the Israelite consciousness evolved from earlier tribal traditions,
and crystallized under the influence of diverse pressures, the fact
is that Israel appears from the beginning as an ethnico-religious
entity. That, at least, is how the Bible wishes to present things,
leaving it to modern Old Testament scholarship to dig out the
complex pre-history underneath the already considerably systema-
tized theological account in the Scriptures. Of course there are
many other instances of identity or near-identity of ethnic, viz.
national consciousness and religion—even in universal religions.
Spaniards find it hard to think of Spain without Catholicism.
Moroccans and Libyans would resent any attempt to define their
identity without Islam, and Buddhism is considered an essential
element of their character by Thais and by the Sinhalese of Sri
Lanka. But in the Jewish case the matter goes far deeper. Perhaps
Hinduism provides a faint analogy, although there the structure
of the relationship between society and its religious culture is
conceived very differently. Judaism is not a case of a religion
arising somewhere and then influencing, impregnating and shaping
a people. The people and the religion have grown together, the
religion not only proclaiming beliefs and dictating behaviour
which the people adopt, but imposing these very specifically on
that particular people as its vocation, life-giving purpose, and
guarantee of existence. Without baptism or faith in Christ there
are no Christians and no Church, and without a sangha and
without individuals taking refuge in the Triple Gem there are
no Buddhists (unless you join in the modern game originated
by Humpty Dumpty, in which a Christian calls Buddhists

'unconscious Christians' and Buddhists may return the compliment by calling every decent Christian an unconscious Buddhist). But even the most orthodox Jewish theologians—as, indeed, also the ancient prophets—would agree that even without faith and practice there was a Jewish people, though they would be quick to add that without faith and practice the people were betraying the ground of its existence and therefore doomed.

This situation has its liabilities as well as its assets. On the debit side, from the religious point of view, there is the danger of cultivating the religious heritage as a kind of national or ethnic folklore, valuable because it helps to safeguard a sense of historic continuity. It has been said of nineteenth-century *Kultur-protestantismus* that what it cultivates is not Protestantism but a pious reverence for Protestantism's past. A similar quip could be made, *mutatis mutandis*, with reference to modern Judaism. The name of Ahad ha'Am is the first to spring to mind when mention is made of modern, secular 'culture-Judaism', but that of Mordecai M. Kaplan is no less significant from a sociological point of view. Kaplan's 'Reconstructionism' which considers Judaism as a cultural social totality is perhaps not a major formative influence, but it is surely a symptomatic expression of much contemporary Jewish life. In fact, it could be argued that much of what is called Judaism both in Israel and in the Diaspora is a series of variations on the Kaplanian theme, often coupled with a determined effort to dissimulate this fact. We shall encounter a very similar problem in our discussion of Islam. If Judaism is what Jews believe and do, then we are not really invoking the theological category of *ijma'*, but rather evoke the cultural and (pseudo-) historical category of *jinsiyah*, or even *jinsiyah 'urfiyah*. One cannot help thinking, in this connection, of the wording of the Declaration of Independence of the State of Israel in 1948. The religious groups insisted on an explicit reference to the Lord God of Israel. The secularists adamantly refused any of the In-God-We-Trust stuff. Being narrow-minded and honest like all militant secularists, they preferred a break with historic continuity to what would have been to them hypocrisy. The final compromise allowed the 'Rock of Israel' into the document —a beautifully vague and evocative biblical phrase which to the orthodox simply means God, and which also the secularist can accept as a poetic metaphor suggestive of the *genius populi* and of the historic continuity, survival and creative strength of Israel. Indeed, a sober study of the cultural and educational policies of the State of Israel may almost create the impression that they were designed specially to illustrate the thesis of Durkheim that in religion society reifies, projects and worships itself. Almost—but not quite, because it might just be that even the secularist is involved in a genuinely religious undertaking when he commits himself, in his own secular way, to furthering the continued life of his people and to what biblical prophets and later theologians called 'an eternal covenant'.

This brings us to the credit side of the ledger. The fact that Judaism is the religion of a people—not in the sense of being a religion that happens to have been adopted by a certain people, but an essential dimension of its national identity—renders a (temporary?) retreat into secular forms possible. No doubt Jewish theology has a lot to learn from the urgent and passionate questionings of the Christian Honest-to-God theologians. But it will have to struggle with these problems in the framework of the given, historical reality of a people. If there is one thing that Judaism does not need, it is the gospel of a 'conversion to the world'. Judaism was always *in* this world, even when dispossessed of it, exiled and ghettoized; its *Torah* conceived of the world as the area of responsible historical life, and of social and political action incumbent on a people on whom God had imposed such responsibility. For unlike the Church which is a metaphorical 'people', and unlike the *umma* which is no people but embraces many, the Jews are an historical people even though their theologians taught them that they were also more. The *corpus historicum* was also a *corpus mysticum*: in the language of rabbinic theology it was called *keneseth Yisra'el* (the *ekklesia* of Israel). For all we know it may not have been Zionist nationalism that represented a 'deviation' from traditional Judaism but the denominationalism which post-emancipation Jewry tried to imitate from Western Protestant civilization. No doubt the problems posed by modernity have been tackled very inadequately, if at all, by Jewish theology, and secularization in the sense of emancipation not only from religious institutions but even from ultimate religious legitimations is a challenge that has not yet been met. Yet, as we have seen, there is at least one aspect of secularization which creates no basic problem for Judaism. Judaism did not have to 'discover' the world. It had its business in this world, though it had to find its way back into the world after centuries of forced seclusion. This is, of course, oversimplifying to a dangerous degree, since Judaism, too, had its other-worldly trends. Even *Torah*, in spite of its reference to the 'world', could be given an other-worldly direction in the ideal of *Talmud Torah*. But by and large it could be said, in the words of Professor J. Neusner (1971, p. 64):

The heavens tell the glory of God. The world reveals His holiness. Through *mitsvoth* [the divine commandments] we respond to what the heavens say; through *Torah* we apprehend the revelations of the world. Judaism rejoices, therefore, at the invitation of the secular city. It has never truly known another world, and it therefore knows what its imperatives require.

This, of course, is a thoroughly theological statement which well expresses Judaism's matter-of-course relation to the world, but does so in thoroughly pre-modern terms. What 'holiness' does the 'world' 'reveal'? And what do the heavens say, if they say anything? The heavens may declare the glory of God, or so at least the Psalmist thought, but—as Sir Arthur Eddington observed long ago—the astronomer can know nothing about it. At about the same time that Friedrich Gogarten published his influential manifesto of secular theology (*Verhängnis und Hoffnung der Neuzeit. Die Säkularisierung als theologisches Problem*, 1953), an American Jewish philosopher, Horace M. Kallen, gave his message in a book entitled *Secularity is the Will of God* (1954). For Kallen secularism is not only 'a development of religion' but 'equivalent to religion itself' and it includes democracy, pluralism, tolerance—in short, all the American virtues. From a theological point of view this is obviously making things a bit too easy, yet it is significant that Kallen, as a typical Jewish non-radical liberal, advertises his version of secularism by legitimating it as the will of God—a most unsecular and unmodern formula.

I have referred in previous lectures to the existence of several apparently similar, undoubtedly related yet essentially different pairs of opposites, such as sacred-profane, religious-secular, ecclesiastical-secular. The meanings of these terms can change (e.g., when secular becomes 'truly' religious, or when 'religious' is un-Christian, or un-Jewish, or otherwise pejorative), and the whole conceptual scheme may be altered as we translate from the language of one culture into that of another. At the present moment we are concerned with the language of Judaism, and we shall go—as, indeed, one should do in the study of all religions —to its most revealing and authoritative expression: the liturgy. The ritual performed on Saturday evening after sunset, at the termination of the Sabbath, speaks of God as He 'who distinguishes [or separates] between the holy (*qodesh*) and the profane (*hol*), between light and darkness, between Israel and the Nations, between the Seventh Day and the Six Days of Labour'. It is an extremely interesting formula. The tension between holy and profane is invoked as a backdrop for the distinction between the Sabbath (as a holy day of rest) and the days of labour which are precisely the 'secular' sphere of temporality that has to be actively sanctified. And it can be sanctified only by active, sanctifying labour in secularity and not by holy rest. The Sabbath may serve as an ultimate and eschatological symbol of a world redeemed, fulfilled, and devoid of dialectical tensions:

> O quanta qualia
> Sunt illa sabbata
> Quae semper celebrat
> Superna curia.　　　　(Peter Abelard)

But in the human world of history it can be said that where

everything is holy nothing is holy, precisely because the sacred exists only in dialectical relation to the non-sacred. We need not discuss here the kabbalistic speculations regarding the possible redemption and 'reversion to holiness' of even the demonic and evil. (These kabbalistic speculations are the Jewish counterpart of patristic discussions of the question whether the devil could be saved.) Suffice it to say here that on the ordinary levels of the Jewish perception of life, secular means that which is there to be sanctified. This tradition has coloured the attitude to the world and to worldliness of most Jews. For the religious Jew it describes the quality of that mode of existence which, under the dispensation of Revelation (i.e., *Torah* and *mitsvoth*), lies between Creation and Redemption.

The last sentence, with its evocation of the triad Creation-Revelation-Redemption, was meant as an obvious reference to Franz Rosenzweig (1886–1929), probably the greatest theologian of twentieth-century modern Judaism, and to his major work *Der Stern der Erlösung* (1921). Rosenzweig did not fuss about proclaiming a 'religionless Judaism', but he prided himself on the fact that in his *Stern* the word 'religion' did not occur even once (Rosenzweig 1937, p. 374). Clearly, as a profoundly religious man, Rosenzweig was alienated, like his Christian successors mentioned in an earlier chapter, by the narrowness and the sense of shrinkage conveyed by that term. Long before Bonhoeffer, in the year 1914, Rosenzweig wrote an essay entitled 'Atheistic Theology' (Rosenzweig 1937), which can be considered an anticipatory polemic against the later Death-of-God theology. What Rosenzweig wanted was 'living under God, but without "religion"'. God did not create religion; He created the world, and hence the purpose of revelation is 'to make the world non-religious again' (Rosenzweig 1935, pp. 430-1).

The work of Martin Buber, too, is an unceasing effort at expounding, in ever so many variations and circumlocutions, the quality of a total and 'whole' life which in its wholeness cannot recognize a distinct, discrete 'religious' sphere. The encounter with the divine 'Thou', God, and by derivation with every 'thou', is all-pervasive. In fact, ' "religion" is man's exile' since only in a period of 'the eclipse of God' is a discrete sphere of religion possible at all, substituting itself for the 'lived concreteness' of the totality of being-with-God, viz., of responding to Him. Since what really matters is the nature and the quality of the living total response to all things in all situations, the distinction between so-called secularists and allegedly 'religious' people is meaningless: 'it is not necessary to know anything about God in order truly to intend God'. One could even say that it is not necessary to know anything *about* God in order to know Him. It is not my intention to discuss Buber, nor to ask whether his brand of 'pan-sacramentalism' would not in the long run undermine any and every possibility of sacredness. Least of all shall I enquire here whether Buber's expositions of certain historical manifestations of Judaism are valid as historical interpretations or whether his accounts of, e.g., Moses, the biblical prophets or the eighteenth-century Hasidic movement merely serve (as every religious 'text' does to every religious commentator) as a kind of Rorschach ink-blot on which the interpreter projects his own philosophy. But enough has been said to illustrate the ways in which Jewish thinkers, resorting to the specific resources of the Jewish tradition, have faced the problem of holy (*qodesh*) and profane (*hol*) in relation to the more inclusive as well as the more restricted connotations of the term 'religion'.[1]

The preceding paragraphs were designed to convey an idea of the resources with which Judaism confronts the '*olam ha-zeh* (the 'saeculum'), and to explain why after centuries of seclusion it needed a re-entry into the larger 'world' but no discovery of it, let alone conversion to it. But, as I said before, this does not

---

[1] I do not bother to consider the argument, advanced by some Jewish apologists, that 'Judaism', viz. Hebrew, possesses no word equivalent to 'religion'. This may be true of biblical Hebrew, much as it is true of classical Greek and Latin (or of Chinese and Japanese, for that matter), all of which have a varied vocabulary related to religion, but no one word that would be precisely equivalent to the sense in which the term is currently used in European languages. And the Hebrew language, like Hebrew and Jewish culture, has not only a biblical dictionary; it also has a history.

E

dispose of the radical challenge of modernity. This-worldliness can be pursued with thoroughly religious legitimations, as theologians know from their canonical texts and sociologists know from Max Weber. In traditional Jewish language these elements of legitimation are called Creation, *Torah*, *halakha*, God's will, and the like. There undoubtedly are forms of modernization that can be effectively pursued with pre-modern means and by means of what I have called traditional coding devices. We shall encounter more examples of this as we look at Islam and some eastern religions. In the Western world there is a considerable number of Jewish writers trying to think in a modern style and in a modern terminology. Their efforts were sometimes marred by apologetic tendencies (including apologetic aggressiveness) and by a somewhat glib adoption of changing intellectual fads. One of the few really interesting and impressive theologians of secularism was the late Abraham ha-Kohen Kook, Chief Rabbi of Palestine (d. 1935). Kook, of whom I like to think as a kind of Jewish counterpart to Muhammad Iqbal, was a curiously audacious Talmudist and Kabbalist, by which I mean to say that he tried to formulate a theology of secularity and modernity in the categories of a pre-modern tradition. At times he would conceal his pre-modern conceptual apparatus and attempt to use what he thought to be a modern vocabulary—however alien it was to his intellectual universe of discourse—in the fond hope of thereby 'getting across' more successfully to a secularized audience. Rabbi Kook was also a theological chauvinist, but unlike his successors he was able to spiritualize his chauvinism in a manner that renders it religiously significant though not necessarily more attractive. Kook was convinced that everything that was true, right and spiritually meaningful ultimately derived from Judaism—including such apparently 'ungodly' phenomena as secular socialism, atheistic materialism, and modern enlightenment. These movements, misunderstanding their true essential nature, outwardly presented an irreligious or anti-religious veneer, not knowing that their substance was from God. Kook's argument, incidentally, provides another illustration of the standard theological procedure of serving the secularist critics in their own coin. Enlightenment criticism and its successors claimed that they knew what religion was all about much better than did the believers themselves. The theologians, in turn, get their own back by claiming that they possess a much more adequate and deeper insight into the nature of secularism than the secularists.

Kook beheld the unity and harmony of all things in the monistic-hierarchical fashion which neo-Platonism had bequeathed to the Kabbalah. Religion—i.e., what in the terminology of modern sociology would be called 'explicit religion'—had shrunk so much that instead of embracing all, its shrinkage had forced the other God-given values to articulate themselves in dialectical fashion by way of opposition to religion. Explicit religion is wrong by conceiving of itself in too narrow terms. Secularism is wrong by absolutizing itself and failing to see that its own nature and fullness are realized only in the framework of that total divine harmony which the integral theological outlook (i.e., Rabbi Kook's own) can provide. Kook does in a Jewish way what certain proponents of Hindu hierarchical monism do in theirs. Much as Radhakrishnan's Hinduism pretends to understand Islam and Christianity and Buddhism better than do the Muslims, Christians and Buddhists themselves, so also Kook was convinced that he understood the enlightenment, socialism, secularism and atheism more adequately than did their respective protagonists. His theology is a fascinating example of what in the terminology of medieval Japanese Buddhism I would call a twentieth-century *kyō-han*. Whether this traditionalist modernism really comes to grips with the nature of modernity can be doubted. But precisely for that reason it may still play a constructive role in the complex process of the modernization of Judaism.

Judaism being the only major contemporary religion based on the experience of the sacred particularity of a concrete historical people, one cannot help thinking, by way of comparison as well as contrast, of Japan. The Japanese analogy is of interest to us because, unlike the traditional religions of African and other tribal societies which are disappearing fast in spite of some attempts at revival in the interests of ethnic and cultural self-esteem, we are dealing here with a highly literate civilization. Since Japanese society (like Western Jewry) modernized rapidly and in a very spectacular fashion, it provides a favourite subject for all students of modernization. The nature and mechanisms of this modernization, the points where modernization and Westernization diverge, the meaning of secularization in the specific Japanese context—all these are fascinating problems which, however, lie outside the scope of our present enquiry. Relevant to our purpose is the fact that the 'canonical' Yamato versions of the Japanese historico-mythological tradition, such as the *Kojiki* and the *Nihongi*—like the Bible—do not give us an historical account that would reflect all the complexities of the early developments. Instead, they present us with a full-fledged ideological system. The relations of the gods to the community are such that the latter is of an inherently sacral character. This sacrality pervades the whole structure, conceived like a pyramid from Ameterasu-o-mi-kami to Jimmu-Tenno and the latter's imperial descendants, down to the whole people. Like the Israelites who are 'children of the Lord your God', the Shinto parish stands in a relation of *uji-ko* to their local tutelary *kami*. In fact, the whole Shinto system could be called (in an admittedly somewhat loose sense) a large-scale *uji-ko* structure. The State Shinto that was developed after the Meiji-Restoration[1] and which reached its peak in the period during the two world wars may have been a perversion of much that is best in Shinto, but, like every perversion, it perverts something that is there. The doctrine of *saisei-itchi*, the unity of State and Shinto, may be an example of such perversion, but its underlying reality is

---

[1] It should be mentioned for the good order that the term 'Meiji-Restoration' is to be taken in a semi-mythological and ideological sense, and in no way as an historically valid expression. The events to which this term refers were anything but a 'restoration', but they were presented as such in order to enlist the legitimating authority of sacred tradition. The Meiji-Restoration is a perfect illustration of the process referred to above (p. 17) as the selective re-shaping of tradition.

the sacral unity of polity and religion, boosted precisely in the context of a modernizing process. Some of the tendencies discernible in present-day Israel are not a little reminiscent of *saisei-itchi*. There was a period when the supervision of religious sects and churches (Buddhist and others) came under the jurisdiction of one government agency, but the administration of what is loosely called 'State Shinto' under another because Shinto was not supposed to be a religion at all in the denominational sense. It was Japan's official 'civil religion', the expression of the very essence of Japanese identity and loyalty. But Shinto in none of its forms (Imperial Shinto, so-called State Shinto, Shrine Shinto, Sectarian Shinto, popular folk-Shinto) had a universal reference though modern Shinto thinkers believe it has the potential for universalism. The sacrality of the community was given; it was not a vocation and a task imposed. Hence also the division of labour by which a non-Japanese, universal religion, namely Buddhism, came to play such an enormous role and to fulfil so many of the functions—cultural, social and individual—usually expected of, and attributed to, religion. And when the Japanese people were called to respond to a religious vocation of universal significance it was by Nichiren, a curious figure whose intolerant zeal and vehemence make him the closest analogy to an Old Testament prophet that Japanese Buddhism has ever produced. Whilst Shinto thus took care of the dimensions of community and polity (in addition to certain other spheres of life such as fertility and growth), Buddhism provided both the universal reference and the dimensions of what we would call individual religion. Similar considerations could be applied, *mutatis mutandis*, to China where Confucianism, Taoism and Buddhism, whilst often overlapping, often distinct, and often in conflict, exhibited a functional division of labour. A Chinese emperor might be a devout Buddhist and patronize Buddhist monasteries, yet he would be committed to a Confucian ideal of the state and derive his own legitimation from the Mandate of Heaven. Jewish particularity, however, functions *ab initio* within a universal setting, and its symbolic reference-system is unified and integral. Historical Judaism is the affirmation of one particularity; to be more precise, of a sacral particularity; to be even more precise, of a sacral particularity that is a vocation, a command and a promise, and that in all its particularity has a universal ground (namely a universal God) as well as a universal reference. Its incarnation in the concrete historical life of a people constitutes that dimension of 'secularity' which makes Jewish thinkers assume, perhaps overconfidently, that their tradition possesses the resources necessary for dealing with modernity. The assumption is, of course, incapable of proof, for even if Judaism modernizes 'successfully', this success (whatever the criteria adopted for measuring it) may be due not so much to specific elements in the Jewish tradition as to structural characteristics of tradition as such, of modernity as such, and of the dialectical interplay between the two. The issue is discussed elsewhere in these lectures and need not, therefore, be repeated here. But what, for the sociologist, is a cultural manoeuvring with a limited number of options is, for the religious believer, a personal matter of vital significance. Diaspora Jewry, being in the main denominationally or pseudo-denominationally organized, as well as the Jewry of Israel with its more all-embracing social, cultural and political concreteness, still have to work out an adequate religious response to modernity. But the concreteness of Jewish historical existence will not permit this response to be an academic exercise of professors of theology. Rather, in the words of E. Borowitz (1970) which constitute an explicit rejection of all apologetic modernism, the primary goal for Jewish thinkers 'has become Jewish authenticity in modern expression, rather than modern justification of acceptable aspects of Judaism'.

Progress and Stagnation: the Dilemmas of Islam

The notes of decline, stagnation, decadence and even degradation are sounded whenever there is discourse on the subject of Islam in the modern period. There is little difference, in this respect, between non-Muslim historians of religion, Muslim modernists earnestly searching their hearts and the resources of their faith, and Muslim (or should I say lapsed Muslim?) secularists accusing Islam of all the evils to which their societies are prey. This sense of stagnation and decline has been with Islam since the fourteenth century at least, and it was this depressing awareness that prompted Ibn Khaldun, the father of historical sociology, to his reflections. The Islamic world that surrounded Ibn Khaldun was, in the words of Professor M. Mahdi (1964) in his classic study of a classic author, 'a spectacle of chaos and desolation'. The onset of that decline is usually dated to the thirteenth century, or more precisely to the fall of Baghdad in 1258, but there seems to be general agreement that the second crisis, that of the modern period, constitutes a far graver and more unsettling threat. According to Gibb (1970, pp. 128-9),

the dangers to which Islam, as a religion, is exposed today are perhaps greater than any that it has faced in the past ... The most patent [dangers] come from those forces which have undermined, or threaten to undermine, all theistic religions. The external pressure of secularism, whether in the seductive form of nationalism, or in the doctrines of scientific materialism and the economic interpretation of history, has already left its mark on several sections of Muslim society. But even this, however insidious its influence, is probably less dangerous in the long run than the relaxation of the religious conscience and the weakening of the catholic tradition of Islam.

Gibb seems to take it for granted that the modern age is inimical to all religion: every religious heritage is threatened by 'the corroding acids of our age'. Gibb's description, whilst in part too simplistic and perhaps too much formulated in a Western style, certainly manages to compress into a few sentences some of the major problems of modern Islam. Let us note that Gibb here refers to the dangers besetting Islam as a religion *stricto sensu*. For certainly Islam is first and foremost a religion—at least, it should be considered as such by the historian of religion. But Islam is also both more and less than a religion. It is a civilization, and as such its problems are twofold. There is the problem of the viability of religion on its own terms: how can what Clifford Geertz has called 'the machinery of faith' continue operating with the traditional orthodox concepts of God, of a unique historical revelation, of the unique sacredness of the Qur'anic Scripture, of a legal system that not only sets ideal norms but also provides in detail and by divine ordinance for the content of the system? But there is also the disturbing and perhaps supreme test of religion on the communal, civilizational and ultimately political and historical level. In Islam this is a genuinely *religious* problem and not merely a matter for neo-Weberian sociologists interested in the interrelationship between religion and the other dimensions of social life, economics, polity and culture. In fact, the more religiously committed you are, the more agonizing the problem, as is movingly demonstrated by the work of such eminent Muslim scholars as, e.g., Fazlur Rahman, who combine historical erudition with theological seriousness, and intellectual sophistication with profound honesty.

For the historian of religion the development that turned Islam into what it is, is one of the most fascinating stories. Here we have a religious message starting out with an eschatological fear of the day of judgment and originally designed to ensure the salvation of the individual believer. Yet before long it not only created a community but also developed a theory about the nature of community in all its dimensions. 'Islam is a religion not only of the moral imperative, but of that imperative embodied in the norms and way of life of a Community that embraces in principle all self-confessed Muslims' (Gibb 1970). In the words of W. C. Smith (1957, p. 39):

Islam is essentially a religion, and as such profoundly personal and also finally transcending all particularities and the confines of this mundane world and all its affairs; nonetheless it has been distinctively characterized by a deep concern for these affairs. It has had a central conviction that the true Muslim life includes the carrying out in this world of the divine injunction as to how mankind, individually and corporately, should live. It has been characterized equally, therefore, by an intense loyalty towards its own community. At its fullest, this conviction has risen to the vision of building the ideal society.

It is precisely this outlook that provided the historical basis which led Muslim thinkers, such as Ibn Khaldun, 'to reflect upon Islam and the Islamic community as a political regime'. As Professor Mahdi (1959) puts it, 'in Islam it is doctrinally essential that religion should not merely have an external concern with worldly affairs . . . or clearly distinguish between affairs of the Spirit and affairs of the World. None of these would suffice. Religion itself must be politicized'. This ideal remains valid even if it was never or only rarely fully realized. This non-achievement is mirrored in the history of the relationship obtaining between 'ulama and rulers—a relationship ranging from non-co-operation to pragmatic (though only rarely opportunistic) collaboration. How much scope, one wonders, does this ideal leave for secularism let alone for the religiously inspired secularism found in contemporary Christianity as discussed in a previous chapter? The Muslim would say that Islam, precisely because of its comprehensiveness, needs no theology of secularization. But this reply would merely be begging the real question.

The criterion by which every religion explicitly or implicitly accepts to be judged, namely by its fruits, includes in the case of Islam also the social and communal fruits. The situation has been analysed with profound empathy and understanding by Professor W. C. Smith in his remarkable and often moving study of modern Islam. Smith sees Islam as 'one of the world's two chief large-scale endeavours to implement a social ideal'. Indeed, Islam and Marxism 'have much in common, more than any other religion has in common with Marxism, with the partial exception of Islam's prototype, Judaism'.

Smith analyses how and why political, historical and social failure is far more critical in Islam than in Christianity. Whereas 'Christianity is supremely a religion of adversity'—the Constantinian legacy notwithstanding—a salient characteristic of the early history of Islam is overt success. The formative centuries of Islam were 'of temporal as well as spiritual achievement... The success was comprehensive as well as striking... the enterprise gained not only power but greatness... The success was of an Islam creative and responsible... not only prosperous but original and constructive. They brought into being a new civilization. The success, moreover, was religious. The Muslim achievement was seen as intrinsic to their faith.' Bearing the cross of adversity and humiliation is, therefore, something that cannot be accepted lightly in Islamic terms. Students of both religion and political science will confirm that this statement is borne out by Arab (Muslim as well as secularist) responses to the defeat (the 'setback') in 1967, as well as to the 'success'—no matter whether real or in military terms illusory—in the Middle East war in October 1973. The crisis is compounded when—as in the modern period and unlike the age of Ibn Khaldun—the religious foundations of Islamic civilization are called into question not only by historical decline and stagnation, but by the explicit challenges of secularism and modernity. On this point, too, I cannot do better than quote once more from Professor W. C. Smith. Religions can, at a pinch, live with their ideals unrealized and their dreams unfulfilled, and failure in this respect is not necessarily disruptive. 'It is when the ideal seems to become meaningless, the dream insignificant or obstructive, that trouble descends. Religiously one can cope with historical developments that are an obstacle to the realization of one's ideal, more easily than with an ideal that is clearly an obstacle to one's historic development '

These profound, and profoundly relevant observations, although made with reference to Islam, apply to all religions in the modern world. Before addressing ourselves more specifically to some of Islam's specific predicaments, a few remarks of more general bearing may similarly be in order here. I have referred in a previous chapter to the traditionalist tendency, present in many religions, to deny change or somehow to explain it away. Conversely, one of the characteristics of modernity, viz. of the absorption of modern value orientations, is the acceptance and even praise of change. As regards religion, this situation leaves three options on both the analytical and the ideological level. Religion can be a catalyst of change (as it has sometimes been in the past) and even of modernization (as the Weber thesis claims for Protestantism). Where change of a modernizing nature is at a premium, theologians will proclaim and advertise their particular brand of religion as the agent of change *par excellence*. We saw examples galore in our previous discussion of modern Christianity with its proliferating theologies of hope, revolution, secularity, liberation, etc. A positive attitude towards change is often surreptitiously recommended by the use of a loaded vocabulary, e.g., by describing a religion as 'dynamic', the implication clearly being that 'static' is a pejorative word. If possible religion should be represented as generating change and renewal through its own dynamics. If this is too difficult, then at least some *deus ex machina* (or rather *ex historia*) arranges for a renaissance to take place. Conversely, if religion is recognized as obstructing change or modernization, then this recognition automatically becomes, in the hands of ideologists, an accusation or even condemnation. We shall soon look at a few Muslim examples. The third option is to admit the incapacity of religion to generate modern change, but to claim that it can respond adaptively and creatively to change. This possibility, too, must be studied on two levels. On the analytical level we are back in what I would call the Weberian universe of discourse. As regards the ideological level, the historian of religion will have to pay special attention to the varieties of ways in which religions claim to, and/or in fact do, integrate innovation. (For an example cf. Bellah 1965). It is not always easy to separate the two levels, and it is even more difficult to decide—perhaps the very attempt to do so is illegitimate—whether religious justifications of modernizing change are genuinely religious phenomena, naïve or glib apologetics (with or without *mauvaise foi*), or simply exercises in jumping on the bandwagons of the *Zeitgeist*. What exactly is one supposed to think of the arguments of Muslim modernists to the effect that the Prophet, if only we interpret him correctly and in the light of our modern sensibilities, 'really' prohibited polygamy? What should one make of such 'socialist' statements as, e.g., that all unequal distribution of wealth would be solved automatically by a proper application of the rules of *zakāt?* I shall, however, try as best as I can to refrain from evaluative terms and concentrate on what seems to me to be the basic problem.

The basic problem is this. Religion is by its very nature traditional, no matter whether it claims to be rooted in a primordial, mythical past, in an historical event (or events), or in a more generalized and diffuse tradition handed down by the ancestors. Tradition means continuity and, beyond mere continuity, the authoritative legitimation—indeed the 'sacredness'—of central values and symbol systems. Even in radically new religions and foundations it is often possible to discern an explicit or implicit appeal to an antecedent legitimating authority (see above, pp. 4-5). The 'New' Testament is not the only example of a new message being legitimated 'according to the Scriptures' of an antecedent authoritative 'Old' Testament. Christian 'theologies of revolution' are brandishing their Bibles to prove that revolution is a direct consequence of the message of the Scriptures and the Christian *kerygma*. Muhammad, according to Muslim orthodoxy, was not the first prophet but the last: the seal of prophecy. We may put the same idea in different words by saying that tradition in general, and religious tradition in particular, serves not only as the repository of substantive values but also as a coding device for new (emergent, borrowed or acquired) ideas and values, thus rendering possible their legitimate absorption. This can be accomplished by means of a variety of mechanisms, e.g., by 'proving' that these new ideas had always been there, at least potentially and implicitly. On the analytical level we can let the Weberian sociologists worry why India, whose Hindu caste system should inhibit democratic tendencies, does in fact come closer to genuine political democracy than any Muslim state past or present. Nonetheless, on the ideological level any Muslim with democratic aspirations will claim that Islam implies democracy. Whether this sort of claim is made too glibly (as W. C. Smith feels it often is) or not, is not my concern at the present moment. I am concerned with the fact that the claim is being made, and I am concerned with it not because we are discussing democracy but because we are trying to understand the relationship between tradition, continuity and change.

I shall leave for later the other alternative: legitimating change by a rejection—actual as well as symbolic—of tradition in what is sociologically the type of the 'cultural revolution'. In these instances change is legitimated by a total commitment to revolutionary norms (which, of course, does not mean that the historian may not subsequently discover the persistence of traditional elements). But short of this radical step, tradition will always be a more or less conscious point of reference—with ambiguous results for religion. For whilst conservatives may hail the preservation of at least some religious traditions, there also is the other side of the medal: religion ceases to be what it was in terms of faith and of the authenticity of the symbolic cosmos in which men of faith lived and moved and had their being, and becomes a cultural element to be invoked, mobilized and often manipulated in the name of cultural continuity and of national and ethnic identity. It is one of the ironies of this situation, and of the necessity to manipulate traditions in the interests of cultural policy, that 'the defence of religion falls upon men who are themselves godless' (Yalman 1973). Islam, Hinduism and Buddhism have developed their own versions of, and analogies to, the nineteenth-century Western *Kulturprotestantismus*. But evidently religion changes its character when it becomes part of the national and cultural concern with continuity. Gibb (1970) still argued in strictly religious terms and in terms of the 'spiritual roots of life and action' when he described the dilemma posed by the fact that 'no Muslim people can shut itself off from the modern world, nor on the other hand sever its spiritual roots in the historic Community and remain a Muslim people in any effective sense'. For Muslim societies the problem is (much as *mutatis mutandis* for Judaism and its *halakhah*) the *sharī'a* no less, and perhaps even more, than theological doctrine. The *'Ulama* or *fuqaha*, like their orthodox Jewish counterparts, are the servants and not the masters of a God-given law which they have to interpret, apply and administer. They can also 'develop' it—provided they do so within the manoeuvring space granted them by that same law. They cannot, if they are faithful and genuine in their orthodoxy, rise above their *sharī'a*, *fiqh* or *halakhah* and question the very nature and basis of its authority and relevance. Hence their most 'progressive' rulings, demonstrating how traditional law can be applied to modern conditions, have a quaintly medieval-scholastic character. Orthodox rabbis consider it a major triumph of progressive casuistry to mitigate the prohibition of shaving by 'proving' that the biblical-rabbinic prohibition applies to knives, viz. blades only and not to scissors (and hence not to most electric dry-shavers which operate on the scissors principle). The milking of cows is not permitted on the Sabbath, but an electric milking machine can solve the problems of an orthodox dairy farmer, provided the mechanism is set by an electric clock on Friday, before the beginning of the Sabbath. Similarly the capacity of Muslim law to come to grips with our technological age has been triumphantly demonstrated by a ruling of the Doctors of Al-Azhar to the effect that *hajj*-pilgrims, who are supposed to don the special white pilgrim's robe on approaching Mecca, may now do so at their home airport before boarding the plane to Saudi-Arabia. The outsider may smile at these expressions of 'modernity', but the student of religion had better understand the full dimensions of the problem and respect the integrity of the expositors of a law who refuse to turn Allah's guidance into mere folklore or—even worse—into a set of 'ritual symbols', the authority, applicability and continued relevance of which is determined by the arrogant judgment of the 'progressive' modernist. But clearly the traditional legal system cannot persist —neither in its details nor in its basic conception. Yet Gibb correctly says that 'if the Sacred Law is wholly dethroned the link with the historic Community is broken'. But saying this is tantamount to inviting the sociologist to take over from the student of religion, or at least inviting the student of religion to become more of a sociologist.

Mention has been made before of the capacity of religion to turn from the present to the future by invoking the past. The logic of this procedure—in terms of the history of Western Christianity it could be called the Reformation Procedure—is evident. If you want to break away from a present which is deemed to be decadent, stagnating or at any rate inadequate, and you wish to do so without staging a cultural revolution, then you must set the discontinuity which you are about to create (or to recognize and legitimate, since it already exists) within the framework of a larger, more encompassing continuity. This is done by judging the negative present as a departure from the genuine, authentic tradition, and claiming to re-establish a more legitimate continuity by returning to the sources. Hence 'modernization' and 'traditionalization' are not mutually exclusive (as Milton Singer (1972) has demonstrated again in his study on South India), and 'modernism' and *salafiyyah* are two sides of the same Islamic coin. In fact, 'scripturalism' is the easiest strategy—at least temporarily and at the initial stage, before its inhibiting powers become fully manifest—for legitimating rejection of the more immediate past.

At this point a further interesting dilemma arises, requiring careful study and abstention from hasty generalizations. Modernization may, as has just been said, require scripturalist purism. On the other hand the commitment to national identity and cultural self-assurance may demand the cultivation of popular tradition and folklore. U Nu's Buddhist revival in Burma paid almost as much attention to the *nat* as to the Buddha. Rabbinic purists may object to the all but pagan popular celebration of Lag ba'Omer at Meron, but cultural policy puts a premium on folkloristic rites. The Islamic version of this dilemma is the hostility to Sufism exhibited by all scripturalists as well as modernists of the *salafiyyah* and *Manār*-type (so-called after the journal edited by Rashid Rida) and, on the other hand, the role of diverse forms of Sufism not only in popular piety from Morocco to Java but also in the theology of some more sophisticated modernists such as Iqbal. One might, in this connection and with a view to the role of *Wirtschaftsethik* in Weberian sociology, also mention the economic success of the Ismailis and the extraordinary case of the Murids of Senegal whose accomplishment is unthinkable without Sufi background and Sufi-type organization. The analogy of the Murid achievement with the Zionist *kibbutz* has been judiciously pointed out by E. Gellner (1973), and his discussion is valuable because it may serve to highlight the difference between what a comparative outlook would call different models of modernization, and what a more narrow Western outlook would unhesitatingly call a difference between genuine modernization on the one hand and pseudo-modernization (viz. religious mechanisms as a necessary transitional device for modern adaptation) on the other.

Scripturalist modernism creates additional dilemmas. As I have mentioned before, religions tend to upgrade the word 'dynamic' whenever they wish to affirm change. The problem of dynamic adaptation is particularly pressing in relation to the *sharī'a*. It is not surprising that W. C. Smith (1957, p. 13, n. 2) should remark on the 'growing tendency to hold that Islam is inherently dynamic, not static', but whatever evidence there is seems to come from India rather than the Arab world. A Muslim writer gave his study on 'Adaptation of Islamic Jurisprudence to Modern Social Needs' the title *Muslims: Decadence and Renaissance* (Mahmassani 1954), yet one is left wondering how much in this title is reasoned judgment and how much is wishful thinking.

J. N. D. Anderson and N. J. Coulson (1967) seem to trust the modernizing zeal of enlightened autocratic governments more than the dynamic qualities of Islam when they conclude their study of 'Islamic Law in Contemporary Cultural Change' with the opinion (p. 92):

In the final analysis: almost everything will turn, during the next few years on considerations of political strength. It seems most unlikely that any process of intellectual and moral enlightenment will significantly change the essential conservatism of the uneducated, or semi-educated, masses in the Muslim world, although a slow evolution of their thought is already taking place. It must be anticipated, however, that it will still be possible for the *'ulama'* to whip up opposition to any change in the law which can be represented as a betrayal of the teachings of Islam—and, indeed, that there will be some of the *'ulama'* fully prepared to take such action—unless this is forbidden by the fiat of an autocratic government, precluded by the influence of a charismatic leader, avoided by the diversion of political enthusiasms into other channels, or countered by the outspoken criticism and comments of the more enlightened of the *'ulama'* themselves.

The case of Tunisia may serve as an illustration of one of the possibilities mentioned in the above quotation.

In many ways Islam seems to present more obstacles to religious modernization than most other traditions—which may be just another way of saying that Muslims may have to work out their own brand of modernity. Some of the principal obstacles should briefly be mentioned here. Islam 'is more reified than any other religion' (W. C. Smith), and as a revelation *from* God rather than *of* God (as Smith once put it) it does not lend itself easily to symbolic translations and transformations. Perhaps Shi'ite and Sufi traditions may have resources that have not yet been fully tapped. Not unrelated to the traditional attitude to revelation and *sunnah* is the strong fixation on the past. Fazlur Rahman's analysis of the kind of Islam envisaged in the defunct constitution of Pakistan as 'essentially past-oriented' (as opposed to, e.g., Communism which is future-oriented) could well be applied to many expressions of contemporary

F

Islam in general. There is not even the pretence of 'dynamic' adaptation, since Islam functions, in the constitution analysed by Rahman, as a limiting concept. As such it indicates what is inadmissible or undesirable, rather than acting 'as a positive or creative factor whence positive results are derived as values, goals or programmes for human progress and enrichment' (Rahman 1970b). This backward-looking limitation is nowhere more evident than in the great modernists. It is no accident that the average reader or student finds it easier to appreciate medieval writers and thinkers than their late nineteenth- and twentieth-century modern successors. In fact, few things appear to us so quaintly, and at times even grotesquely, old-fashioned and out-dated than yesterday's 'modernism'. Much of this quaint archaism is due to the fact that modernists like al-Afghani and Abduh never really understood 'the radical character and the explosive possibilities of the new challenge' (Mahdi 1959). Their reforming modernism was basically naïve, in fact unmodern. Even Iqbal, with all his glorification of modern science (though not of the modern European civilization with which it went), with all his ardent commitment to the notion of history, and with all his Sufi-cum-Nietzsche-cum-Bergsonian philosophy, would see in modernity a return to the original intention and nature of Islam. The modern revolution is thus no genuine revolution at all, but the conscious and full acceptance by Muslims of their true heritage. This is the message of Iqbal's *Reconstruction of Religious Thought in Islam* (1934), and such is, in one way or another, the 'answer' offered by every modernist apologist. With less radicalism and less genius than Iqbal, other modernists simply and somewhat glibly proclaim that all truth, including all modern scientific discoveries, can be shown to be contained in the Qur'an. The less sanguine writers more modestly claim that all truth is compatible with the Qur'an or that the Qur'an, dealing with religious truth only, leaves other areas free and autonomous in search for truth. This view may seem very similar to some Western conceptions of secularization, but in the Islamic case it is not so much the result of a genuine struggle as of a failure to come to grips—as yet—with the real challenges of modernity. The '*ulama*, for all their learning and realism, are least 'educated in modernity. They therefore cannot give a lead in the community's . . . great task . . . of coming to terms with that modernity' (Smith 1957, p. 286). Meanwhile modernists expound their modernism by writing commentaries on the Qur'an. If you are socialist, anti-capitalist and anti-Western (as if socialism was any less Western than capitalism and colonialism!) you will have no difficulty in demonstrating that the cradle of socialism was in the Qur'an and in early Islam.

One of the causes of this failure—and perhaps symptom as much as cause—is the impossibility in many parts of the Muslim world to air these problems in open and frank discourse. As W. C. Smith (1957) puts it, 'official censorship on the one hand and, doubtless more important, the unceasing pressure of fear and the (often hypocritical) forms of social conservatism and vested prejudice, preclude open discussion'. As an illustration one may quote the sneering remark of a radical, and in many ways brilliant, Marxist anti-Islamic firebrand, Jalāl al-Azm, addressed to another secularist, positivist and naturalist but non-Marxist critic of religion, Nadīm al-Bitar. Al-Azm pillories the failure of Muslim society to permit criticism of Islam—and, after all, according to the prophet Marx 'criticism of religion is the premise of all criticism'—with the derisive comment: 'Nadīm al-Bitar can permit himself to write as he does because he lives in Canada!' And sociologists know the difficulties of obtaining reliable information on religious beliefs and observance in Muslim countries by means of the usual questionnaire methods.

Before turning to the forms of radical, positivist or Marxist, criticism of Islam, brief mention should be made of one important aspect of Islam that I have neglected so far. Together with Buddhism and Christianity, Islam is one of the world's great universal religions. Universality in a religion creates its own problems. Universalism (as has been pointed out in a previous chapter) is almost, by definition, universalistically exclusive. It tends to be intolerant of particularities, and even more so of competing universalisms. Even at its most tolerant, its tolerance is of a complex and involuted character. Nevertheless, in actual historical and social reality, the universalism of a religion has never prevented the development of a sense of identity of religious culture with national character. This is true of Spain no less than of Thailand. I shall not discuss Pakistan in this connection for the latter is, in the words of F. Rahman (1970b), an 'ideological state' which possesses no other common element but Islam to weld the many disparate groups into some kind of national unity. In the case of Bangladesh even Islamic unity was evidently not enough. In most Arab Middle Eastern states, however, Islam is the expression of a cultural tradition as well as national character, and it is not surprising therefore that from Egypt to South Yemen and from Morocco to Iraq, Islam is explicitly recognized as the state religion and the *shari'a* as the 'source of legislation'. An interesting ambiguity arises here in the Arab world, for, of course, as a universal religion Islam is theoretically as much Malaysian or Pakistani or Senegalese as it is Arab. The universal aspect of Islam is brought out very movingly in the autobiography of Malcolm X (1965), whose experience of the Hajj finalized his break with Muhammad Elijah and the American Black Muslim movement. We may ignore here, for our present purpose, some interesting features of Malcolm X's account: the childish elation of the kid from the black ghetto at the flattering (and perhaps calculated) hospitality of his hosts, or the simplistic naïveté with which the dichotomy black (= good) *versus* white (= evil) is shifted from skin complexion to social attitudes and behaviour. The important point for our present argument is not that Malcolm X now identified evil with 'Western' (i.e., 'white' now becomes a metaphor for Western attitudes), or that he simply ascribed colour discrimination in the Muslim world to Western influence. (Bernard Lewis's paper (Lewis 1970) on the subject had not yet appeared at the time, and even if it had, Malcolm X would surely not have taken any notice of it, or, alternatively, dismissed it as another wicked Western ploy.) My point is that Malcolm X suddenly realized that as a Muslim he could not be a racist. Hatred had to be deflected from an ascriptive object (white skin) to an oppressive, exploitative and discriminatory social and cultural system. On the other hand there is no denying that 'Arabism' (not only in the very special role of the Arabic language as the language of the Qur'an) plays a unique role in Islam and that, conversely, Islam plays a very special role in the consciousness and self-image of the Arab peoples. This much can be affirmed without going to such grotesque extremes as expounded in Ismail al-Faruqi's disconcertingly strange work—one would almost call it a theological paroxysm —*On Arabism: 'Urubah and Religion. A Study of the Fundamental Ideas of Arabism, and of Islam as its Highest Moment of Consciousness* (1962).

In an age of de-colonization, new states, and political independence of old societies, the flourishing nationalisms of the day pose a serious problem to a religion such as Islam. Gibb (1970) seems to consider 'the seductive form of nationalism' as one of the ways in which secularism threatens to undermine religion. Indeed, nationalism is rejected by the *salafiyyah* type of thinkers who I think could best be described as 'modernist fundamentalists'. I do not know whether Abduh and Rida had ever heard of *Kulturprotestantismus*, but they very clearly rejected *Kulturislam*. *Al-din* in the sense of ethnic identity or of the religious culture of a community (*jinsiyah*) is a perversion of its meaning and contrary to true Islam. 'Our course is this *tafsir*'—says the Abduh-Rida commentary on the Qur'an, the *Tafsir al-Manār*, on Sura III, 360–61 'has been a rejection of making *al-islām* a conventional ethnic identity (*jinsiyah 'urfiyah*) heedless of the fact that it is a divine guidance'. Similarly Sayyid Qutb, one of the leaders of the Muslim Brotherhood, executed by the Nasser regime in 1966, speaks in his commentary on the Qur'an of 'the flag that *al-islām* raises in order to save mankind from the fetters of partisanship to *al-jins* [nationality], and to the world, and to clan, and to family'. We are, in fact, taken back again by these utterances to the familiar tension between nationalism and pan-Islamism, since Qutb explicitly states that 'the Muslim is not established as an individual except in a group'. But precisely for that reason Islam sets up 'the banner of God—not the banner of patriotism. And not the banner of nationalism. And not the banner of *jins*. All of these are false banners which *al-islām* does not know'.

Perhaps more than any other Muslim thinker, Muhammad Iqbal not only felt the tensions of this dilemma but also exhibited them. Iqbal is counted among the spiritual fathers of Pakistan, and he, like Sir Sayyid Ahmed Khan, has been called a religious chauvinist (Dean 1959, p. 35). Iqbal's poem *Shikwa* and his *Huseyn Ahmed* should be read together: a Muslim can have no nation but Islam (see W. C. Smith 1957, p. 283). But perhaps the most serious moral dangers, from the point of view of Iqbal's religiosity, are posed in equal measure by nationalism and atheistic socialism. His words deserve to be pondered by Muslims and non-Muslims alike (p. 188):

Disappointed of a purely religious method of spiritual revival . . . the modern Muslim fondly hopes to unlock fresh sources of energy by narrowing down his thought and emotion . . . Both nationalism and atheistic socialism, at least in the present state of human adjustments, must draw upon the psychological forces of hate, suspicion and resentment which tend to impoverish the soul of man.

Disappointment with the role of religion in social and spiritual renewal invites one of the obvious alternatives: radical anti-islamic secularism. Integral orthodoxy and even 'selective orthoxy' (in Professor Y. Harkabi's happy phrase) are out. Your commitment is no longer to tradition but to 'reason', or to a thoroughly revolutionary ideology. The Turkish example so far provides the most complete model of consistent secularism in a Muslim (though, we should add, non-Arab) society. It also illustrates the resilience of religion after years of radical seculariza-tion. Whilst I do not believe in the so-called 'religious revival' in Turkey—what happened was simply that the traditional religiosity of the people freely expressed itself again as soon as permitted to do so by a more liberal regime—the fact remains that awareness of Islam as a dimension of Turkish identity reasserted itself in the context of a secular polity. The violent anti-Islamic diatribes of the early Turkish secularists are now taken up—albeit in a more contemporary Marxist style—by some Arab modernizers. Nadim al-Bitar's hotch-potch of Nietzsche, Camus, Julian Huxley and the radical theologians (he quotes Bonhoeffer, Hamilton, Altizer) culminates not in the Western-style obituary notice 'God is Dead', but in the passionate appeal that 'Allah must die'. Not being a vulgar all-out Marxist, al-Bitar sees no need to condemn Islam as *ab initio* reactionary, feudal, exploitative, superstitious and the like, but adopts a more relativistic and historicist line of attack. Religion was an adequate ideology for yesterday; today it is an anachronism; and to the future-oriented revolutionary who today anticipates the world's tomorrow, it is clear that Islam must give way to a positivist naturalism. Al-Azm is no less radical. Unless Islam is destroyed and the religious superstructure of Arab civilization brought down, there will be no renewal. For once Europe is held up as a model: European progress began with a revolt against religion. 'History is the graveyard of ideologies' (al-Bitar)—excepting, of course, Marxism which is the eternal *evangelium veritatis*. As an amusing sidelight it may be mentioned here that al-Azm was for some time a best-seller on the Palestinian West Bank, and that the Muslim authorities there, who in general studiously refrain from any contacts with the Israeli occupying authorities, turned to the then Prime Minister, Mrs Meir, with a demand to exercise censorship and to ban the circulation of al-Azm's writings!

Both Muslim modernists and anti-Muslim secularists bear witness to the magnitude of the Western invasion. Islam did not generate modernization but—like other Asian and African societies—experienced it as an invasion from outside. The values espoused—no matter whether in an emotional framework of xenophobia or of xenophilia—were Western. Some modernists appropriate these values simply by claiming that they had always belonged to the Muslim heritage. In fact, genuine values cannot be genuinely Western, because the West stands for technical superiority but spiritual underdevelopment. We should not underestimate the significance of this cliché. It is, of course, a favourite Third World slogan, reiterated not so long ago by the present Secretary-General of the World Council of Churches, but propounded already in 1894 by Swami Vivekananda when explaining to his disciples in Madras that, as India was deficient in social virtues, so America was deficient in spirituality. 'I give them spirituality; they give me money.' This syndrome is not exclusive to the Third World, and many an orthodox Western rabbi has expressed his conviction that Judaism had nothing to learn from Western and/or Christian civilization, though it should not hesitate to profit from Western technology. Muhammad Iqbal thought much the same. Reference has been made more than once, in the preceding chapters, to the ambivalence of non-Western reactions to the Western impact, as well as to the fact that 'Christianity' and the 'West' often appeared to be identical. The progressive secularization of the West has had a double effect. It enabled Christianity in non-Western societies to de-Westernize and 'indigenize' itself, and it enabled secular trends to reject Christianity (and the values of the colonial, liberal and nineteenth-century civilization in general) as 'Western', whilst espousing the communalist, anti-individualist and socialist values of the present as 'indigenous' because less clearly identifiable with the nineteenth-century forms of Western influence. Only arch-conservatives still persist in denouncing all socialism as 'Western', but all forms of non-Western defensiveness are simply the obverse side of Western arrogance and aggressiveness. The general problem has been posed, in lucid and thoughtful terms, by Professor Bernard Lewis (1964, p. 43):

from time to time in recent years Middle Eastern thinkers have put the question: what is the result of all the Westernization? It is a question which we of the West may well ask ourselves too. It is our complacent habit in the Western world—the more so the further west one goes—to make ourselves the model of virtue and progress. To be like us is to be good; to be unlike us is to be bad. To become more like us is to improve; to become less like us is to deteriorate.

It is not necessarily so. When civilizations clash, there is one that prevails, and one that is shattered. Idealists and ideologues may talk glibly of a 'marriage of the best elements' from both sides, but the usual result of such an encounter is a cohabitation of the worst.

The apologetic response of presenting Islam in modern garb easily invites irony and sarcasm, e.g.: 'The modernist wishes to demonstrate that his religion is respectable, relevant, and as up-to-date as this year's new car or the latest fashion. Islam is described as the bearer, even the originator, of liberal values which today are cherished in most enlightened societies.' This description is applicable to other religions too—to some brands of Christianity no less than to certain versions of Buddhism—but what is referred to as 'today' has meanwhile become yesterday in many parts of the Islamic world. Ali A. Mazrui (1966-7) attributes the disproportionate number of Muslim countries among Africa's radical states to 'the Islamic defensiveness in relation to Christianity, interacting more recently with nationalistic opposition to Western imperialism'. The new modernity makes new forms of compromise possible:

What is making a reconciliation even more probable is that twentieth century modernism, unlike that of the nineteenth century, is not immediately identifiable with Christian civilization ... The wave of the future in the nineteenth century seemed to be the civilization of self-consciously Christian countries. But the wave of the future in this century includes a form of socialistic radicalism that is, at times, anti-Christian. The successes of the Soviet Union and Communist China do not confront a Muslim with the same psychological problems that the successes of Christian Europe used to do.

Mazrui feels that the 'deep-seated defensiveness which Islam has towards Christianity continues to have an effect on the nature of Muslim radicalism today'. There are, no doubt, areas of the Muslim world 'which remain almost untouched by modernity. But where there has been a Western impact of some significance, that old defensiveness of the Crusades is there, ready to be roused again'.

The defensiveness against the West enormously complicates the responses of Islam to modernity. One of the simplest reactions has already been mentioned: whatever is good and desirable had always been Muslim, even if for some time it has been 'lost' and had to be recovered again from the West. Only that which is irredeemably bad and to be completely rejected deserves to be called 'Western'. The secularist, on his part, is echoing Western ideas to an even greater extent, but as a secularist he cannot simply islamicize them. Concepts like the death of God, or secularization, are imported from a culture where they had their natural growth and where they could even function as religious symbols, into an alien climate and an alien soil. One should not force questions deriving from one religious culture on to the universe of discourse of another. But since al-Bitar and others enthusiastically quote Bonhoeffer, Hamilton and Altizer, the observer may be permitted to ask whether a Muslim Bonhoeffer and a 'religionless' Islam, in fact, whether a Muslim 'radical theology' are possible and, if so, what they would be like. This is precisely the question asked by an Arab Jesuit critic of al-Azm, Father Bulus Nuwayya. Writing in *Mawwāqīf*—a periodical edited by another modernist, of a different kind, who expounds his brand of existentialist and half-mystical secular modernism under the significant pen-name ADONIS—Father Nuwayya judges al-Azm's thinking to be philosophically poor and his arguments against religion to be superficial. Their significance resides in the light they shed on the situation of contemporary Islam. Al-Azm's *Naqd al-fiqr al-dīnī* is an important *document humain*, or rather *document culturel*, illustrating the split which the invasion of Western modernity has produced in the Arab soul. Father Nuwayya concludes that Islam stands in need of a Bultmann and a Paul Ricoeur (a significant tribute to the *formation française* of Catholic theologians in the Lebanon!); it wants re-interpretation and de-mythologization.

This, of course, is the big question, and the above account does not lack certain grotesque features. A Western intrusion into Muslim civilization is countered by al-Azm with a Western-type revolutionary programme, and an Arab Catholic theologian prescribes a Western-type theology as remedy! Surely from an Islamic point of view this may appear as an attempt to cure one evil with a greater one. I do not know how representative al-Azm is of tendencies in the Muslim world and how influential. As a matter of fact I do not even know the extent of Iqbal's influence. Iqbal is an impressive figure by any standards, and he has his quota of admirers among Western students of Islam. He has also left his mark on many Muslims in the Indian sub-continent. But how significant his brand of modernism will turn out to be in the long run is still difficult to assess, precisely because Iqbal never really faced the true dimensions and full reality of 'modernity'. He, like other modernists struggling at the frontiers between tradition and modernity whilst the world sped on to its post-modern phase, often appear to us as so pre-modern. Yet for all we know, sociological retrospect may show that this is one of the most efficient methods of dealing with modernity.

Recognizing that Islam, as a religion, has not yet really met modernity, let us reflect in conclusion on the central symbol of Islam: *la ilāha illā Allah, wa-Muhammad rasūl Allah*. The first part of this testimony links Muslims with the traditions of all mono-theistic religion. The second half expresses the historic specificity of Islam. Western Christians indulge, as we have seen, in secular theologies, considering these as the most modern, contemporary and up-to-date versions of the theological game. Will Muslims be able to show that their faith, as well as their city, follow other models and paradigms, and are not necessarily amenable to the Western dichotomies? Western theologians speak of the death of God with a cheerful, glib and triumphant sense of tragedy, sheltering themselves behind the Maginot Line of their refurbished *ad hoc* Christology. They do not de-mythologize but thoroughly re-mythologize, i.e., project their own, allegedly more modern myths of an existential and/or social and/or secular kerygmatic Christ. The way to this manoeuvre is barred to the Muslim. *La ilāha illā Allah:* if God is a myth, then one has to live with this myth, for there is no *Stellvertretung* and no substitute myth to take its place. Will Islam as a religion be able to proclaim the *shahāda* in a modern and post-modern age, testifying against both Western notions of secularism and Western theological acrobatics? Alas, the spectacle of contemporary Islam is not merely one of stagnation but actually of regression when compared to the creativity, vitality and capacity of positive absorption and transformation which Islam exhibited in its golden ages. Contemporary Islam seems to lapse more and more into fundamentalist orthodoxy—a phenomenon not unknown also in other religions, but with the crucial difference that at the other end of its spectrum Islam lacks all genuinely modernizing dynamisms. The essentially unmodern, but at least in its intentions modernizing 'modernism' of earlier modernists seems to have spent itself before reaching the point of take-off into real modernity. Much apparent self-assertion of Islam is the product not of a genuinely religious awareness but of anti-Western affects and, not infrequently, of lip-service to Islam by those who are far removed from religion but for whom Muslim identification is a convenient idiom for Arabism or for Third World militancy in general (cf. e.g., the wholesale rejection of Western 'orientalist' scholarship by many Muslim 'orientals'—including the allegedly westernized ones—who should know better). And at the other end of the scale Islam inevitably becomes the object of a complex and involuted anti-Islamism. The challenge of modernity is mighty, and the resources of Islam may be exhausted. Or are there resources still untapped and awaiting release? Between resurgent literalist fundamentalism, anti-western affects, nationalism and secularism, Islam will either disintegrate or turn into *jinsīyah*, unless it can re-assert itself as a *dīn Allah* for a modern age.

Affirmation Through Renunciation:
Dharma, Moksha and *Nirvana*

'*Namo Tassa Bhagavato Arahato Sammasambuddhasa*—Homage to the Exalted One, to the One of Supreme Worth, the perfectly Enlightened by Himself.'

This traditional, semi-liturgical formula of veneration may serve to remind us, though no reminder is really necessary any longer, that Buddhism is, as all Buddhists agree, a religion, the occasional disclaimers of earlier theistic philosophers and some Buddhist modernists notwithstanding. Among the latter we should perhaps even count no less an authority than Alexandra David-Neel—apparently the first to have coined and used the expression 'Buddhist modernism' (David-Neel 1911)—who described Buddhism as an 'a-religious philosophy' as distinct from occidental irreligiosity.

It has been customary for a long time among students of religion to distinguish between Western and Eastern religions not merely in a geographical but in a typological, viz. phenomenological sense. Since all great living religions have come from the 'East' (at least when viewed from a European perspective), the border between East and West is drawn somewhere near the Indus river. The Western religions—which would include Judaism, Zoroastrianism, Christianity and Islam—are described as 'prophetic', more active, and oriented towards this world, society and history. The Eastern religions are said to be more mystical, ascetic, a-historical and world-negating. Like all generalizations, this one too is helpful up to a point, but up to a point only and hence at the same time also very misleading. It draws our attention to certain important traits which we should not lose sight of, but stated in a simple, generalizing way the distinction is at best a half-truth. And a half-truth is, by definition, also a half-untruth. It is not only the tremendous variety among Eastern religions, and within each and every one of them, that makes generalization risky, but also the similarities obtaining between *prima facie* very different religious systems. I shall have to say something later about the view, advocated more especially by some modernist Hindu thinkers, that all religions are essentially one and only outwardly appear to be different. Whatever the merits or demerits of this philosophical and theological doctrine—for it is that, and certainly not a generalization derived from an empirical study of the historical religions—students of religion tend to be far more impressed by the truth of an opposite observation, to the effect that religions, however different they may be in their origins, fundamental insights and doctrinal structures do, in fact, tend to become similar. This phenomenon was forcefully pointed out not by a professional historian of religion but by a British psychologist, Robert Thouless (Thouless 1940, p. 1). Nobody would dream of denying the differences between Christianity and Buddhism, but they are not terribly relevant when comparing the behaviour of a pious Catholic passing by a roadside cross or shrine, and that of a pious Buddhist passing by a temple or stupa. The sangha is certainly something very different from Christian clergy; yet occasionally their functions and roles are disconcertingly similar.

In the little time at our disposal we shall try and look briefly at two great Indian religions, or rather religions originating in India: Hinduism and Buddhism. To obtain some insight into their similarities and divergencies one could do worse than begin with an analysis of the word *dharma* and its meanings in the two systems respectively. We may, in due course, return to the concept of *dharma* but at present I should like to start out with a consideration of the allegedly world-negating character of the Indian religions.

Let us recall what has been said in a previous chapter about the partly analytical and partly ideological functions of certain terms—'loaded' terms as they are. This-worldliness is a case in point. It was used by the Church-fathers and later Christian polemicists as a stick to beat Judaism with (as long as other-worldliness was considered to be a superior, because less materialist, form of spirituality) or, conversely, as a convenient Jewish stick with which to beat Christians (when this-worldliness rated higher). In an age when this-worldliness and the 'secular' relevance of religion are at a premium, the student of Comparative Religion may amuse himself with discovering the standard Jewish criticisms of Christian world-negation in some modern Christian discussions of Hinduism and Buddhism (see also below, p. 94). Suddenly it is no longer the carnal mind of the Jew, but the prophetic and kerygmatic nature of the Christian faith that chides Buddhist world-negation in what I have called before a game of theological one-upmanship. No less a man than Archbishop William Temple alleged that one of the great failings of Buddhism was that in order 'to safeguard both the reality and the supremacy of the spirit, it dismisses the material as illusory'. And when Western scholars want to be nice and to earn the applause of their Eastern friends, then they bend over backwards to prove that Hinduism and Buddhism are not really all that world-negating as alleged by other (and evidently mistaken or prejudiced) Western critics.

It is unnecessary to emphasize that no religion is really and totally 'other-worldly'. If it were, it would not survive its founder, let alone succeed in creating social structures, shaping cultures, and producing historic continuities. The question therefore has to be rephrased: what is the nature of the 'dialectical' mechanisms by means of which certain forms of world-affirmation are legitimated through ultimate values that define themselves as 'other-worldly'? For the latter, somewhat abstract formulation we could, in our present context, substitute the specific terms *moksha* and *nirvana*.

Donald E. Smith (1963) has characterized the difference between Hinduism and Buddhism as one between 'metaphysical tolerance and social rigidity' on the one hand, and 'social freedom and ecclesiastical power' on the other. Without quite subscribing to this terminology, let us begin with the metaphysical tolerance and social rigidity side.

The Hindu case is remarkable as it presents a society completely permeated by religion. This religious ordering of society without a church or ecclesiastical organization, and without clergy or other centralizing institutions, is of great significance to comparative studies, quite apart from causing very serious headaches to Indian politics and religion. One merely has to think, in this connection, of the legislative labour pains in giving birth to temple reforms (e.g., the various state legislations, the Lok Sabha debates in 1960, or the Hindu Religious Endowments Commission Report of 1962), or of the controversies surrounding the creation of an 'Indian Sadhu's Association' (the *Bharat Sadhu Samaj*). The European experience originally posed the problem of secularization in terms of separation of church and state. The American experience has shown that you can keep church and state strictly separated whilst increasing the symbiosis of religion and society. In the Hindu case secularization can, in the nature of things, never mean the separation of the state from a non-existent church; it will mean the extrusion of traditional religious rules, structures, practices and ideas from the life of the society in which they had been lodged. The state, instead of being charged with preserving the sacred heritage, is now charged with preventing the latter from interfering with the ordering of society as conceived by modern values. This can be accomplished in diverse ways. Objectionable religious customs (e.g., animal sacrifice, *devadasi*) would be attacked by modernist reformers for being incompatible with the 'true' spirit of religion, i.e., the attack is launched in the name of what is held to be a superior and more authoritative value-system. Certain social institutions may be declared to be 'mere' customs that have grown in history and that can therefore also be abolished in the course of history. On the other hand human ingenuity knows no limits to the wrong-headed resourcefulness and sophisticated perverseness with which it can rationalize any tradition or custom: a study of the literature and the agitation generated by the 'holy cows' can serve as a very instructive exercise in this respect. Since time immemorial the caste system has been considered to be of the essence of Hinduism. Already the laws of Manu (second century, B.C.) lay down—according to Dandekar (quoted by D. E. Smith 1963, p. 294)—that 'obedience to caste rules is the very essence of *dharma*'. We are not concerned here with the role of the concept of *karma* as an instrument of rationalization of this particular *dharma*—Weber called it 'the unique Hindu theodicy of the existing social, that is to say caste, system'—but with the *dharma*-character of the system as such. This particular 'essence of *dharma*' is of interest to the student of religion because it is endorsed—for very different reasons, of course—by both Hindu conservatives and anti-Hindu critics. The late Dr B. R. Ambedkar insisted that caste was inseparable from Hinduism. Hence social progress had to be non-Hindu. It is not surprising that Buddhism should have lent itself as the most natural 'Indian' (i.e., non-Western) idiom of *harijan* protest, and as recently as 1973 the Dalai Lama administered initiation to 4000 *harijan* at a mass conversion ceremony in New Delhi. When a descriptive sociologist, Dr Srinivas, opines (D. E. Smith 1963, p. 297) that 'if and when caste disappears, Hinduism will also disappear', then orthodox Hindus as well as anti-Hindu critics will heartily agree. Objections would come from Hindu religious reformers—of the type of Ram Mohan Roy, Dayanand Sarasvati, or Swami Vivekananda —bent on proving that caste was not essential to religion. In due course Gandhi, too, adopted the position that caste was simply a custom that had nothing to do with religion proper, and S. Radhakrishnan even undertook to provide a Hindu philosophical justification for rejecting the caste system: since all individual souls are part of the same Ultimate Reality, it was only logical that the ultimate unity of all beings in the Absolute should be reflected in social equality.

No doubt the modern notions of equality as well as their extension to democratic conceptions regarding the social and political order, appear more blatantly 'Western' when manifesting themselves in a Hindu context. In actual fact they are no less

Western in a Muslim or Buddhist context, but these latter—unlike Hinduism—can more easily invoke traditional elements and texts to validate, as it were, egalitarian tendencies. Western influences are evident in most Hindu reform movements, and few students would want to quarrel with von Glasenapp's description of them as efforts to combine Indian and Western values (Glasenapp 1928). The operative influences derive from 'European science, European spiritualism, European Christianity, European philosophy, European social ethics and European methods of propaganda', and they fuse with 'Indian exegesis of the Vedas, Indian techniques of meditation, Indian ritual, Indian cult of gurus, Indian nationalism and Indian ethics'. Von Glasenapp also notes the practical and activist re-interpretation of a-cosmist Vedantism, and concludes, with considerable sociological insight, that 'however odd these attempts at creating systems by combining Indian faith and superstition with occidental science and pseudo-science may seem to us, there is no doubt that this road . . . in spite of its imperfections . . . can lead to a future'. It is unnecessary to specify here the influences that helped to shape, e.g., Aurobindo's philosophy or Gandhi's social ethics.

If there is one element in the Indian tradition that can claim to lend itself more easily to linkage with modern secular values it is the notion of the secular state. The almost Macchiavellian character of the *arthashastra* tradition of political thought, the ancient Indian 'art of statecraft', has often been remarked upon. According to K. M. Panikkar (quoted by D. E. Smith 1963, p. 61) it propounded 'a purely secular theory of state, of which the sole basis is power'. Now we must not, of course, mistake Kautilya's political theory for political reality, or overrate the actual influence of the *arthashastra* and make light of the *rajadharma* tradition. In this connection it may be useful to remind ourselves of the fact that Indian doctrines of divine kingship flourished especially in Buddhist kingdoms (after undergoing appropriate emendations). Even a minor Buddhist monarch would be conceived—in symbolic theory—as a *cakravartin*, and this notion would be further 'buddhicized' by regarding him as a *bodhisattva*.

Buddhist courts would maintain brahminical priests for certain, clearly indispensable, royal rituals, especially coronation rituals, but the notion of divine kingship exerted its influence also in an opposite direction: from political ideology to Buddhist cult. Few tourists admiring the richly clad and bejewelled Buddha statues in Bangkok realize the full extent and significance of this transformation of the monastic renouncer to a universal ruler, the demonstration of which was one of the most brilliant scholarly feats of the late Paul Mus (Mus 1928). Hindu sacred kingship, on the other hand, should not be exaggerated, for, as A. L. Basham (1954, p. 86) has put it: 'divinity was cheap in India. Every Brahman was in a sense a god, as were ascetics with a reputation for sanctity . . . If the king was a god on earth he was only one among many, and so his divinity might not always weigh heavily upon his subjects.'

Caste and kingship have briefly been mentioned in the foregoing not merely because of their interest to questions of egalitarianism and the secular state, but because of their relevance to more fundamental issues. The caste system reflects a hierarchy of values, and at the top of this hierarchy is renunciation of the world. Renunciation has several functions. It is the one traditionally sanctioned way to break out of the rigidity of the system with its rules of purity, caste and the like. The *sanyasin* is above and beyond; he can opt out of the system because he opts out of the world, and *sanyasa* could therefore be considered, perhaps not altogether wrongly, as a kind of safety-valve. It is a permanent social possibility, re-asserted as such by Buddhism, whereas Hinduism somehow mitigated it by integrating its slightly anarchic possibilities into another rigid social theory. Renunciation, as the way of life of the old man, was absorbed into the framework of the biographical temporality of the four *ashramas*. More relevant, however, to our present purpose is the element of *sanyasa* present in the concept of Brahminism. The Brahmin is at the apex of the social pyramid of values. He cannot—in theory at least—share in power, but without him the king cannot legitimate his power. The Brahmin needs the king's gifts, but the king needs the Brahmin's acceptance of his gifts. The Brahmin can fulfil his function precisely because he occupies a 'dialectical' position at the frontiers of transcendence, between relationship and non-relationship, between interdependence and the total severance from all things inherent in the ideal of renunciation. The Brahmin is, in a sense, part of the social structure; but at the same time he paradoxically embodies the idea of disengagement from it. It is inadequate, therefore, to describe his function as simply 'priestly', especially as the 'kingly' role of the ruler originally involved many priestly functions and responsibilities. Within the 'Brahminic complex' the element of *sanyasa*, as one of its institutionalized value dimensions, is no less decisive than that of priesthood. *Mutatis mutandis*, much the same could be said for the 'functional equivalents' to Brahminism implicit in certain aspects of the social role of the sangha.

Hence India, in addition to the patterns and mechanisms of modernization encountered everywhere, also exhibits its very specific and individual variations. Mention has been made in previous chapters of the tendency to re-valorize and even renew ritual and other traditions as a means for bolstering national self-esteem and a sense of cultural dignity. In the case of Hinduism and the Indian national movement the first and obvious example to come to mind is that of Tilak and his revivals of religious traditions (e.g., the annual Ganpati celebrations) for nationalist purposes. The rediscovery of Hinduism as a reformable and modernizable yet nonetheless traditional Indian religion helped to build self-esteem. So did the admiration for Indian religions, and Eastern wisdom generally, exhibited by Western enthusiasts. The ambivalent feelings of inferiority gnawing away at the Indian soul were compensated by the flattering reverence paid by the Madame Blavatskys and Annie Besants. (It may be mentioned here in passing that in 1973 Buddhist Sri Lanka (Ceylon) formally commemorated the 66th anniversary of the death of Colonel H. S. Olcott). Negative elements in the religious and cultural tradition could be dismissed as perversions and inessentials. Positive elements could now be identified as not necessarily

Western but 'truly' Indian, and referents to elements of modern culture could thus be identified in the tradition. Gandhi's charisma was inseparable from his image as a *sanyasin*. The social emancipation of lower classes and castes often proceeds by way of a process frequently called 'Brahminization' (or 'sanskritization'). Caste became one of the major determinants of the emerging voting patterns in the functioning of Indian democracy.

The modernizing role of traditional elements is, of course, no proof of their actual modernity or abiding relevance. Very often the mobilization of traditional resources in the modernization process is a phenomenon of transition, marking and assisting the passage from a pre-modern to a modern stage. To use a Buddhist parable: once it has reached the shore of modernity, a society may find that it need not remain attached to the ferry. Some elements of modernity could be discovered in the Indian tradition—at times by means of (to put it mildly) forced and arbitrary exegesis; other forms of modernization were facilitated by certain structural elements of tradition. Occasionally the modernization process appears to risk perpetuating that which it intends to abolish or to change: this, at least, is the complaint of some critics of the Scheduled Castes Act.

From a religious, as distinct from a purely sociological point of view, one might say that Indian secularity has creative scope precisely because on the one hand it knows of a *dharma* as a pervasive, guiding norm, and, on the other hand, it locates all legitimation in a transcendent sphere where alone liberation can be achieved. The *dharma*—to quote Louis Dumont's variation of the well-known definition of constitutional monarchy—rules but does not govern, and the ultimate sanction and legitimation of whatever is done on the 'lower' (historical and social) plane, i.e., on the levels of *kama*, *artha* and *dharma* derives, at least in theory, from a sphere that is beyond all this, the sphere of the liberation of man's essential self, a sphere of which renunciation is the means and the witness in this world. But things are not that simple. Secular modernity means that legitimation and ultimate sanction are no longer sought in a transcendental realm; they are part of the reality which has to be legitimated. Will Indian 'monism' provide the tools for a possible answer?

The dialectic of renunciation and involvement is even more marked in Buddhism. We shall have to neglect here the Mahayana forms of Buddhism where problems are very different in view of the actual historical and social realities as well as of the doctrinal presuppositions. But Theravada Buddhism, too, is an elusive entity, though our knowledge of it has improved enormously in recent years, and we are now at last able to begin to 'tie in' the different Buddhisms that have resulted from the different approaches. There is the theoretical, philosophico-religious Buddhism based on a somewhat one-sided interpretation of the so-called canonical scriptures. In my private jargon I refer to it as B.P.S. (i.e., the Buddhist Publication Society in Kandy) Buddhism. A study of this Buddhism, however, no matter how scholarly and edifying, will not give you a clue to what makes a Burmese, or Thai, or Sinhalese village 'tick'. The philological and philosophical study of the canonical texts has now happily been supplemented by anthropological field work, as well as by research concentrating on the social and political aspects of Buddhist history. Different scholars have introduced different terminologies in order to distinguish the various types and levels of Buddhist 'precept and practice', and to analyse the ways in which doctrines and realities interact. Thus Bechert (1966) distinguishes canonical, traditional and modern forms of Buddhism. Sarkisyanz (1965) speaks of scriptural, political, and popular forms. Spiro (1970) distinguishes a normative-soteriological ('nibbanic'), a non-normative soteriological ('kammatic') and a non-soteriological ('apotropaic') system within Theravada Buddhism. A most instructive illustration of these distinctions is provided by the fact that Ashoka's famous edicts (as Paul Mus 1965, p.x, has pointed out) have ever so many references to *dharma*, but never once mention *nirvana*. The important thing is to realize that in actual fact the 'dialectic of practical religion' functions far more harmoniously than analytical distinctions, let alone doctrinal abstractions would lead us to suspect.

Nevertheless, doctrine must not be neglected, for only its uncompromising affirmations enable the 'dialectic' of practical religion to be truly dialectical. It is hardly necessary to point out once more the social functions and involvements of the sangha. The point to be emphasized here is not the 'priestly' and teaching roles of the monks—so obvious and well known that we may take them for granted—but the complex network of reciprocities (giving *dana*, accepting gifts, acquiring merit, making the acquisition of merit possible) which creates what could be termed the 'magnetic field' of sangha and laity. Our present concern is with the fact that the sangha functions the way it does precisely because in theory it is totally 'outside'. Bhikkus are, theoretically, not the equivalents of a Christian teaching order, or of an order of Brothers of Charity dedicated to nursing the sick, let alone feeding the hungry—since it is they who have to be fed and are precluded from providing for their food save by begging. In fact, it is far more meritorious to feed a fat monk than a starving beggar. And as for systematically performing acts of mercy, 'he that would be an *arhat* should not do good deeds'. This saying reminds us of the aforementioned Hindu equivalents: the *sanyasin* who has renounced everything (*samnyasa*) *ipso facto* also renounced all action (including action productive of merit and of good *karma*), whereas the others practise at best *karmayoga*, implying the renunciation not of action but of the fruits of action. In fact, the *Bhagavat Gita* (18.2; see also 12.11) uses a special term for this latter less strict and less specific type of renunciation—*tyaga*—to distinguish it from *samnyasa*. If it is 'for Mara to tell' what good works are required (because 'good works' are viewed primarily from the angle of the accumulation of merit rather than that of 'social action'), then one begins to understand why the charge of 'selfishness' came to be levelled at Theravada Buddhism by both Mahayana and Christian polemicists. 'Its love is self-love; its peace self-conceit and indifference to the suffering of others.' Thus wrote, seventy years ago, the Reverend H. P. Cochrane in his autobiographical *Among the Burmans: A Record of Fifteen Years of Work and Fruitage* (1904). The same worthy missionary also predicted that modern science, by destroying the mythological cosmology of Buddhism, would ultimately sweep away the whole system. The author of this rash prophecy could hardly have foreseen that theologians of his own faith would soon set an example in the noble art of 'de-mythologizing' and of ridding religious traditions of their obsolete cosmological ballast so as to make the pure light of their message shine, not through a pre-modern glass darkly, but face to face with what was supposed to be modernity. There is no need here to record the Buddhist replies to Christian accusations of selfishness; the most violently polemical can be found in Vijayawardene's *Revolt in the Temple*, and most of the relevant material has been assembled by Sarkisyanz and Bechert. More germane to our present theme than the missionary accounts of the Buddhist ethos are its allegedly more value-free descriptions by historians and sociologists. Winston L. King (1962b) rightly states that in the 'common view Buddhism could not possibly produce a social or political ethos, or inspire political action'. This 'common view' has been enunciated in more pontificating style by Christopher Dawson (1948) who argued that religions of pure contemplation were in danger 'of a divorce from historical reality and from the social order which deprives it of spiritual efficacy and creativity in the order of culture'. The famous phrase in the Prajnaparamita Sutra 'gone, gone to the other shore' is considered by Dawson to be also 'the epitaph on Buddhism as a living and creative religion . . . Thus the world of culture is gradually weakened and finally deserted, like the great Buddhist cities of ancient Ceylon where the jungle has returned and swallowed up palaces and monasteries and irrigation tanks, leaving only the figure of Buddha contemplating the vanity of action and the cessation of existence' (p. 193). Dawson, too, could not foresee that a generation living in the wilderness, the jungle and the ruins of a once–Christian civilization might find in Buddhism some of the 'spiritual efficacy and creativity' of which it stood so badly in need. Already Weber had felt that Buddhist 'indifference' was incompatible with interest in this world, and that Buddhist values

were an obstacle to purely economic goals of rational accumulation, investment and profit. A good illustration of this alleged
quietism is provided by the invocation of the doctrine of *karma* for
the purpose of justifying inaction. Indeed, how can you combine
the notion of *karma* with that of modern planning? One can
sympathize with the wrath of the modernist author of *The Revolt
in the Temple* (p. 133) at the remark of a Ceylonese politician in
connection with the malaria epidemic in 1935: 'The people are
suffering for their *karma*. A government cannot alter one's *karma*.'
Weber who, in a phrase worthy of Marx himself, had described
the sangha as a *Domestikationsmittel* of the masses, also noted the
greater economic effectiveness of Hindu over Theravada social
ethic. Similarly Bechert, than whom none is better aware of the
social and political dimensions of Buddhist history, correctly
emphasizes that *original* Buddhism could not provide legitimations
of political power and of rulers. For the historian, all this does not
mean, of course, that Buddhism cannot creatively shape cultures
and political civilizations. It merely means that the mechanisms
of legitimation and the dialectical interplay between ultimate
value-systems and practical social values follow a different
pattern than that considered by the Panglosses of Western
civilization to be the best. To the modernist all these learned
analyses and distinctions make no sense at all. For him Buddhism
is the most 'modern' religion in the sense that modernity is
scientific, for nothing can be more scientific than Buddhism. As
early as 1896 the Bhikkhu Ashoka (= Gordon Douglas) termed
Buddhism a 'scientific religion', and the *Maha Bodhi Journal* as
well as later apologists of the calibre of Mr Justice U Chan Htoon
or the Ven. U Thittila in Burma, and the late Dr G. P. Malalasekera
in Ceylon never wearied of demonstrating that it was the most—
or perhaps even the only—truly scientific religion in the world.
Writers with a special weakness for modern materialism would
be quick to point out that the latter had long been anticipated
by Buddhism which knew 'more than some modern scientists
and materialists'.

But Buddhist 'science' also has its *praxis*. In the first place

Buddhism is presented as thoroughly political. The Venerable Chief Abbot of the Malwatta Vihara, in his enthusiastic Foreword to *The Revolt in the Temple* proudly asserted (what bhikkhus at other times would have been ashamed to confess *even* if it were true) that 'the Sangha of old not only wielded influence in the election, coronation and conduct of kings and sub-kings, but also, whenever the occasion arose, directed and actively participated in the work of the emancipation of the country and its people'. This paean to the 'political monks' is a far cry from the admission made to me by a venerable Vietnamese bhikkhu to the effect that situations might arise in which a monk was in conscience bound to engage in politics, 'but then he has to disrobe first'. For the author of *The Revolt in the Temple* the sangha was established by the Buddha 'as an organized Brotherhood . . . who had dedicated their lives to the service of mankind' (p. 576), almost like a Catholic charitable order. Indeed, the monks are 'not mediators but only [sic!] leaders' (ibid.).

Political action, however, is only one part of social action in the widest sense, and the latter is sanctioned by Buddhism because Buddhism, so we are assured, is this-worldly. The Buddha's message, so the Anagarika Dharmapala declared in a famous book published in 1913, was a 'Social Gospel', and for D. C. Vijayavardhana (1953) 'a reborn Buddhism . . . would be a Social Religion'. Varying with the predilections and political sympathies of the individual apologist, Buddhism is socialist, Marxist or democratic. The Buddhist assemblies 'were fully democratic' (*Revolt*, p. 595), and the sangha is the 'oldest democratic institution in the world' (Malalasekera 1973, p. 8). Hence it need occasion no surprise to learn that the House of Commons procedure of passing a bill only after three readings had been anticipated by the Vinaya rules. After all, the Buddha had also 'anticipated the UNESCO Charter by twenty-five centuries' (Malalasekera 1973, p. 10). Certainly some Buddhist writers anticipated their Christian counterparts in their flirtations with Marxism. The modernist is not bothered by the fact that from the point of view of the historian, 'the Buddha' was no social reformer at all, let alone a social revolutionary, but essentially conservative (see Bechert 1960, i, pp. 7–8).

At this juncture, and before proceeding any further, it may be useful to enter a parenthesis to the effect that all references to 'the Buddha' should be read as if surrounded by quotation marks, since for the historian there is no possibility of speaking of the pre-Ashokan Buddha. In fact, the 'historical Buddha' is even more elusive and evasive of the scholar's grasp than the 'historical Jesus'. For the modernist, however, the Buddha was a superior proto-Marx even as Ashoka was 'the Lenin of Buddhism' (Vijayavardhana 1953). It is not very difficult to show, even without Max Weber, that Buddhism is incompatible with capitalism and with the values of an acquisitive society. From there it is only one step to the assertion that 'Marxism is a leaf taken out from the book of Buddhism—a leaf torn out and misread'. Democracy is another such leaf, and 'universalist humanism' is the essence of the Buddha's doctrine (*Revolt*, pp. 595–7). All this makes perfect sense if it is assumed that the Buddha (and not Jesus, as the fashionable radical theology of the Christian West has it) 'was one of the greatest rebels in human history' (Malalasekera 1973, p. 12) launching a revolt not only in the Brahminic Temple but also in society. The Buddha as a rebel makes even more sense if it is assumed, at the same time, that Buddhism is this-worldly, 'seeks the meaning of life in life itself', and far from regarding the world as a prison from which man must escape rather seeks 'to build heaven here'. As if to lead this train of thought *ad absurdum*, some enthusiastic modernists went so far as to equate the ideal social order with *nirvana*. The notion of a paradise on earth which could, at a pinch, be justified in traditional terms as a penultimate state, has thus usurped the place of the ultimate, *nirvana*. Hence it is quite possible that not only political considerations but also doctrinal reasons prompted the anti-Marxist propaganda campaign conducted by U Nu's government. Indeed, there is much to be said for the argument used during that campaign that far from restating the truth of Buddhism, Marxism had re-stated some of the errors which 'the Buddha had refuted'.

Much of this modernist and apologetic literature may appear to us naïve and glib at the same time. Often it suggests that the authors have not really come to grips with modernity. The result is an enthusiastic eclecticism which distorts the Buddhist tradition and completely misunderstands the nature of Western culture and modernity. *The Revolt in the Temple* is a curious and brilliant, yet nonetheless fairly representative sample of this type of 'modernism'.

I have not discussed here the role of Buddhism in Asian national movements, but much of what has briefly been said on the subject in connection with Islam and Hinduism holds true, *mutatis mutandis*, also for Buddhist countries. In fact, the role of religion in national revivals is so patent, that one easily understands why a Christian missionary in Ceylon would complain that Asian non-Christians were making 'the most awful hash of nationalism and religion' (*Revolt*, p. 498). But being profoundly conscious of its nature as a universal religion (and the most scientific and humanist one to boot!), modern Buddhism is not likely to be completely submerged by nationalist elements. From the point of view of the outside observer, the significant thing about Buddhist modernism is not so much its aforementioned glib and naïve eclecticism—for there is much more in contemporary Buddhism than that—but the fact that the Buddhist revival is essentially a lay movement. The initiative and drive for modernizing developments emanated, in the main, from lay circles. This is no mean achievement—the Ashokan precedent notwithstanding—if one considers the fact that the standing of the laity in the Buddhist 'church' was doctrinally a dubious matter. Whereas not even the most clerical-minded and sacerdotalist Catholic theologian would ever have dared to suggest that priests and laymen were anything but equal members of the same church and of the same 'body of Christ', bhikkhus were perfectly capable of claiming that Buddhism and the sangha were identical and that the laity had no Buddhist standing at all. The organizational expression of this change wrought by modernity is the World Fellowship of Buddhists. At any rate, a new chapter has been added to the history of the dialectic of sangha and laity.

No doubt the preceding account of modernizing movements in Buddhism was one-sided in more than one respect. It was one-sided not only in terms of the facets of Buddhism on which it focussed, but also in its approach. This approach was deliberate, and inevitably epithets such as 'naïve', 'glib', and 'eclectic' made their appearance. I adopted a narrow, Western perspective when describing the Buddhist response to the Western impact and the resultant problems of modernization, not merely because a Western leopard cannot easily change his spots (especially when these are, as in all comparative and cross-cultural studies, 'blind spots'). The purpose of the exercise was to force on our attention, once again and as crudely as possible, the question of the models of modernization with which we are operating. Is Western modernization the only available paradigm, or do we allow other cultures and traditions to produce their own types and parameters of modernity? If we accept the latter alternative, then the need for a more rigorous analysis of the nature and role of the undeniable Western impact (including also the anti-Western and by implication often anti-Christian effects generated by it) becomes even more imperative. Are religious revivals a genuine element of non-Western (as of some Western) patterns of modernization, or are they a characteristically non-modern idiom which pre-modern civilizations need in order to articulate their modernizing tendencies and without which they cannot effect the transition into modernity, which is then defined as essentially 'secular'? Modernity, and even more so the concept of post-modernity, implies innovation and an increasing capacity to handle innovation. Religion, in addition to being a pre-modern idiom at times blocking and at times assisting the transition into modernity, may itself become modern or post-modern, like the rest of the culture in which it is embedded and to which, at the same time, it stands in a dialectical counterpoint. Whether the future of religion is that of an illusion, or an integral part of the future of post-modern humanity appears to be a question which some writers try to discuss in the sober terms of analytic prediction whilst others seem to prefer the tones of the incantatory magic of self-fulfilling prophecy. But there is no *prima facie* evidence to suggest that the symbolic systems built around *dharma, moksha* and *nirvana* are less capable of coping with the predicaments of post-modern man than are those derived from the biblical tradition.

Is the Snark a Boojum? or Post-traditional Religion: Opium, Sugar-coating and Vitamin

There is a curious undercurrent of tension and emotion accompanying many apparently academic discussions of religion in the modern (or post-modern) age. Underlying these discussions seems to be an anxious preoccupation, explicit or unsuccessfully disguised, with the question of the future of religion. The Baker has met with the Snark of modernity, but is modernity a Boojum? Will religion vanish away, either 'softly and suddenly', or gradually and after a series of spasms and paroxysms (so-called religious 'revivals')? For a great many theologians and sociologists this vanishing is a 'notion they cannot endure'; others think that this vanishing will be no different from the much advertised Marxist 'withering away' of the state. And hence the future of religion is sought with thimbles and care, with forks and hope, or their equivalents.

Our necessarily superficial and fragmentary survey of some religious reactions to modernity cannot pretend to contribute either to the many current attempts at scientific forecasts or to the equally current ideological exercises in self-fulfilling prophecy. We began with a brief consideration of the notions of tradition, secularization and modernity. We discussed the phenomenon of change, and of modernization as a form of change characterized by certain special and novel qualities. We examined the concepts of secularism, secularity and secularization, pointing out that the latter could serve both as a descriptive term referring to certain types of change, and as an ideological watchword. We noted that secularization could be among the factors leading to modernization, but that in other settings the relationship might be the other way round: modernization leads to increasing secularization.

We also noted that the beginnings and the original 'take-off' of these processes were not only specific to the history of the West (and more especially of Western Christianity), but also closely related to a very particular aspect of that history: the enlightenment criticism of religion. Criticism of religion, or at least categories of analysis and a conceptual apparatus derived from the critical tradition have since become part and parcel not only of anti-religious ideologies but also of the modern study of religion, both in its so-called 'value free' and in its apologetic forms. Concepts derived from the criticism of religion became part, first of our scientific terminology, and subsequently even of the self-interpretation and self-expression of religion itself in its modern forms. In this respect there is not much difference between 'secularization', Weber's concept of rationalization, and Marx's notion of alienation. Even though many of our current concepts were originally applied from the 'outside', as it were, and used as a critical, often hostile and deliberately reductionist method of explanation, they nevertheless became, in the hands of theologians, instruments for a normative interpretation of religion from 'inside'. Whether this is making a virtue of necessity or not is, as I have argued before, utterly immaterial. The student of religion must not prescribe to religions how to express themselves; he must listen and record before analysing. Max Weber was certainly no phenomenologist of religion in the sense in which G. van der Leeuw meant to be one, yet his work too is in a sense 'phenomenological' and he certainly insisted on the requirement to see religious phenomena also from the point of view of the actor and not exclusively from the outside as a *chose sociale*.

Our review of the relations of religion and modernity, and of the religious responses to the latter, has shown a diversity that can be reduced to four main types.

There is the view of religion as creating, or at least catalysing and contributing to the emergence of (secular) modernity. We found two main variations on this theme, the one analytical-descriptive, and the other theological-ideological. The most significant aspect of the analytical, sociological version is the recognition of the complete autonomy and independence of 'modernity' as regards its origins. What makes modernity modern is the fact that whilst its genesis may, perhaps, have to be explained at least in part in terms of certain biblical, Christian or Protestant elements, its nature cannot be adequately understood by reference to them. Modernity is modern because it has cut itself loose from whatever religious antecedents it may have. The ideological version assiduously ignores this historical emancipation and insists on interpreting modernity and secularity as expressions and forms of the religious kerygma.

According to another and more modest view, religion, or some forms of it, is not necessarily generative of modernity but at least compatible with it by enhancing the sense of values inherent in certain aspects of modernity, and by providing a symbolic structure of meaning. Because of its openness to transcendence, such a symbolic structure enables modernity to function meaningfully in spite of its limitations. Criticism of religion is integrated into religion as part of the ongoing process of critical ('prophetic') purification of religion. Here, of course, some of the most crucial problems arise, for the question at issue is that of the self-sufficiency and immanence of a modern *Weltanschauung*. What exactly does the modern version of 'openness to transcendence' imply? or—to put the matter differently—is there a human movement of 'transcending' when there is no 'Transcendence'? And if it be replied that the reference is to a non-reified transcendence and that the latter need not be spelled with a capital T, then religions must surely realize that they have reached a critical turning-point in their history.

Others again see religion as more than merely compatible with modernity. Religion can be invoked for the purpose of legitimating modernizing reforms. We have seen how the use of traditional symbols as a coding device can ensure a sense of continuity and of legitimating authority in situations of innovation and radical change. It is the favourite method of reforming religious 'modernists', and our discussion has suggested that religious modernists

H

are essentially un-modern. In fact, the use of pre-modern mechanisms for bringing about modernization or introducing religious reforms presents problems of both definition and evaluation. At present it is still too early to say whether we are dealing with a permanent function of religion or (as seems to be the case with many so-called 'new sects', nativistic revivals, cargo cults, etc.) with a typical phenomenon of transition. There are cultures which cannot pass from pre-modernity to modernity except by way of a transitional religious articulation.

Finally there is the radical view which holds religion to be essentially incompatible with modernity. The dependence of this view on enlightenment criticism is evident. In fact, one could describe its diverse forms in terms of a history of the metamorphoses of this criticism and its increasingly penetrating and increasingly sophisticated forms from Voltaire to Feuerbach to Marx to Freud. The 'idiom of rejection' varies from the moving pathos of Nietzsche's atheism to the bored indifference of much twentieth-century 'irreligion'.

When speaking of alleged incompatibility we must, of course, distinguish between two very different problems. There is the question of the future of the traditional historical religions (however modernized, reformed and reinterpreted). The preceding chapters, whilst not even attempting to answer that question, have tried to sketch the background against which any future answer will be given. The other problem concerns not the historical religions, their institutional forms and/or kerygmatic élan, but religion in the singular. Marx himself seems to have envisaged the possibility of ritual celebrations of the new, liberated and true humanity—something very different both from the utopian 'New Christianity' of the Saint-Simonists whom he so heartily despised and from the manipulative religion which, according to Comte, the philosopher-priests of positivism have to feed to the masses. A more sophisticated and more humanistic descendant of Comte and Spencer who also had the virtue of being himself a great scientist, Julian Huxley, similarly felt that a 'humanist-religion will have to work out its own rituals and its own basic symbolism'. But religion is more than expressive ritual and celebration. It is even more than an attempt to deal with so-called crisis situations. Whatever truth there is in this interpretation may well derive from the fact that these 'crises' (e.g., birth and death) are not isolated phenomena but are themselves 'symbols' of an all-encompassing quality of our existence.

It is precisely at this point that the traditional forms of criticism, so characteristically 'modern', may begin to become antiquated as we move from modernity to a post-modern age. In this respect Marx and Freud have rightly been described as key figures in spite of their dependence on some of the cruder forms of nineteenth-century materialism and positivism. Others would criticize religion in ways that exposed its false reifications (to be cured by de-mythologization) and its alliance with vested interests and iniquitous power structures (to be cured by a social gospel and a revolutionary re-orientation of religion). Marx and Freud attempted to go to the very roots of the religious phenomenon and addressed themselves to its basic problem: why and whence its quality of sacrality. To say, with Durkheim, that the sacred is social is true even though it may not be the whole truth. But this assertion gives us not so much an explanation as a tautologous definition of the social as sacred. It certainly does not account for the peculiar quality of sacredness, but this is precisely what Freud and Marx, each in his own way, set out to do. It is not my purpose here to discuss Marx or Freud in detail, or to summarize the present state of studies concerning their work. But we should at least remind ourselves of the fact that the future of religion was discussed by Freud under the title *The Future of an Illusion* (1927). Unlike Marx, Freud had no utopian optimism to sustain him. Like Marx, Freud realized that religion reflected —as its most revealing symptom—the nature of the human condition. 'To be religious is to be sick, by definition: it is the effort to find a cure where none can possibly exist. For Freud, religion can be only a symptom of what it seeks to cure' (Rieff 1961). As regards Marx, one brief quotation is apposite here, if only because one of its key words re-appears in the subtitle of this chapter. 'Religious suffering is at the same time an expression of real suffering, and a protest against real suffering. Religion is the sigh of the oppressed creature, the heart of a heartless world, and the soul of soulless conditions. It is the opium of the people.'

The word 'opium' is slightly misleading, for according to Marx it is not simply religion that is false and provides illusory comforts. What was false was the human condition of which religion was the correct, adequate and true expression. Religion becomes false as the falseness of the human situation of alienation is recognized and gives way to truer forms of consciousness. But if religion exists wherever there is alienation, then it may perhaps be more permanent than the heroic optimism of Marx allowed. In fact, Marxism itself may be a religion—not for the reasons usually advanced in sociological discussions of secular ideologies as 'substitute religions' and the like, but for a more strictly Marxist reason, to wit that Marxism, too, not only in its institutionalized, party or state forms, is a way of generating and expressing alienation. 'The history of humanity is a history of multiple alienations', differing from each other in their manifestations and structure, but not in their essence. And once Marxism relinquishes its dogmatic totalitarianism, realizes its historical relativity and recognizes the utterly utopian character of its anthropological ideal of total transcendence of alienation, it will all the more readily come to terms with the ongoing relevance of religion. Surely even a devout Buddhist need not— like some of the modernists discussed in a previous lecture— necessarily make a fool of himself by identifying nirvana with a just social order, yet he may commit himself to Marxist socialism whilst realizing that the transcendence of alienation is a transcendent goal rather than the culmination of an historical process. He may even have a name for this transcendence: nirvana. Similar reflections could be made with regard to Freud, and the writings of Erich Fromm are a (not necessarily convincing) example of how a neo-Freudian can rediscover a religious dimension and actually assume the role of a psychoanalytic revival preacher.

We are driven back to the question of meaning and of the

construction of symbolic systems of meaning. Up to a point a discussion of this subject could, I think, be followed also by religious fundamentalists, at least as long as they admit that even God cannot reveal himself to man and be perceived as acting in man's world unless man was a symbolizing animal. The crucial significance of the symbolization process for any discussion of religion is by now a commonplace, and there is no call here for a survey of the development of the concept 'symbol' in modern philosophy since Kant (and up to Ernst Cassirer and Suzanne K. Langer), in romantic thought (including Schelling), in contemporary sociology and anthropology, and last but not least in psychology. Whatever view one takes of the theories of C. G. Jung and of the applicability of his anything but 'scientific' analytical psychology to cultural phenomena, there can be little doubt of the importance of the basically phenomenological and anti-reductionist approach to symbolism which he has bequeathed to psychology. It was Jung's profound respect for symbols that made him remark that a symbol could never be translated—except into another symbol.

Before pursuing the subject of symbolism further, a word should be said on the related question of 'meaning'. All writers dealing in one way or another with symbolism and symbols constantly and inevitably return to meaning and to the construction, both individual and social, of universes of meaning. The big question is, if I may borrow from the title of a once very famous book, 'the meaning of meaning'. This genuinely philosophical enquiry is beyond the present writer's competence and, fortunately for him, also outside the scope of his subject. Is the quest for meaning a 'meaningful' human activity, in which case the continuing relevance of religion is evident, or is it an archaic residue of pre-modern illusion? Is the abandoning of ultimate meanings sheer nihilism? Or should some forms of apparent nihilism be viewed more positively as pathetic protests against pseudo-meanings whose falseness has been exposed, much as *mutatis mutandis* mystical nihilism was an option for the great Nothing (with a capital N!) and against the false or inadequate images of

God? The notion of man as a builder of systems of meaning is a commonplace of philosophical as well as of social and cultural anthropology. In sociology it was one of Weber's basic assumptions, and the theme has been taken up again more recently in the work of P. Berger and Th. Luckmann. Symbolization as an activity constructing and expressing systems of meaning seems to be inherent in the structure of human existence. Why this should be so is a matter for philosophical anthropology rather than for Comparative Religion.

This approach may appear to encourage, or even pre-suppose a thoroughgoing relativism. I doubt whether this is a correct appraisal. But it is certainly incompatible with any kind of dogmatic exclusivism. Robert Bellah (1970) has called this approach 'symbolic realism' as distinct from 'historical realism' on the one hand, and from 'symbolic reductionism' on the other. Perhaps 'historical realism' is not the most felicitous term as it is too much indebted to the Christian tradition with its preoccupation with historical events such as the Virgin Birth or the Resurrection. Since the reference is not only to allegedly historical events but also to other forms of reification of mythological and symbolic statements we should, perhaps, speak of 'symbolic literalism' rather than historical realism. With this terminological amendment, Bellah's distinction seems eminently useful though it requires much further clarification if we want to draw a satisfactory line between symbolic realism and the traditional forms of allegorical-symbolic interpretation on the one hand, and symbolic reductionism on the other. The difficulty is perhaps best exemplified by Jungian psychology which, precisely because of the high seriousness with which it approaches symbols, hovers precariously between a reification of the archetypes and a new reductionist allegorization (i.e., the view that symbols 'really' symbolize processes in the psyche such as the development of a more inclusive consciousness or the emergence of the 'self').

The problem of symbolic relativism arises whenever you deal with symbols only. Religious people, however, believe that although they handle symbols and nothing but symbols, they nevertheless are not engaged in symbolic games. Hence a religious believer is fully entitled to say that not all religious symbols are equally acceptable, equally valid, equally good or even equally 'true'. He may even sense and oppose the danger of a non-committal and almost dilettantish aestheticism. Aestheticism is a kind of sympathetic appreciation, and at times even admiration, of the 'meaningfulness', or 'truth', or 'profundity' of symbols, which however lacks that ultimate seriousness and commitment to authority that makes a religious symbol a *religious* phenomenon. Understandably enough aestheticism is equally repugnant to existentially committed Christians (e.g., Kierkegaard) and to existentially serious philosophers (e.g., Jaspers). These considerations do not, however, detract from the usefulness and the essential validity of the concept of symbolic realism.

The shift to a symbolic understanding of religion as systems of meaning, and the problems it raises with regard to relativism *versus* authentic affirmation, necessitate a brief discussion of what has been referred to in an earlier chapter as *theologia religionum*. The student of comparative religion operates, by definition, from an archimedic point outside religion, though obviously inside some secular, cultural, and possibly ideological system—no matter what religious commitments he chooses to make as an individual believer. Theologians operate from *within* a religious system. Trying to give a reasoned account of their faith, theologians have to consider all relevant aspects of reality, and this reality includes the fact of the existence of 'other' religions. Hence theologians must formulate what their respective religions believe not only about God, the soul, salvation, etc., but also about the other religions. They all have, explicitly or implicitly, a 'theology of religions'. The student of comparative religion has to pay as much attention to this expression of religion as to any other. What Karl Barth, or H. Kraemer, or *Nostra Aetate*, or S. Radhakrishnan have to say about other religions is as much part of their Protestant, viz. Catholic, viz. Hindu faith as are their beliefs about God, or salvation, or anything else. Hence, logically enough, History of Religions was taught in many European

universities in the Faculties of Theology as a subject coming
under the general heading of either Apologetics or 'Theology of
Missions'. Nowadays the general heading would probably be
renamed Ecumenical Theology. 'Other' religions may be considered as sheer idolatry (possibly wicked and immoral to boot,
which is the view the Old Testament takes of ancient Near
Eastern religions); as the halting and mostly misguided quest for
God by that part of humanity that has not been vouchsafed a
direct revelation; as a providential, direct or indirect, *praeparatio
evangelica* and as the activity of the *logos spermatikos*; as legitimate,
natural and primitive expressions of religion, albeit inferior to the
'higher' forms; as manifestations of the mysterious and hidden
workings of God in the hearts of 'other' men and cultures; as
partial and finite ways to the same Infinite One, etc. You can
distinguish between 'peoples of the book' and the others. What all
these have in common is that each view, articulated from within
a particular tradition, assumes its own religion to be the summit
and apex of the pyramid. It is the typical *kyō-han* procedure
mentioned before in connection with Japanese Buddhism. This
holds true also of 'catholic' religions such as Hinduism which
rightly considers itself to be less exclusive than the prophetic
religions. Undoubtedly Hinduism with its 'monistic polychrome'
(W. C. Smith 1957) is far more tolerant than the Western mono-
theistic religions, but it clearly considers itself vastly superior—
if only for the simple reason that it proclaims (at least through the
mouth of its modern spokesmen) the relativity of all finite
ways to the infinite goal, whereas the other (and inferior)
religions think of themselves as absolutes. In other words, this
type of religion holds its own (relative) relativism to be an
absolute yardstick. This view—*honi soit qui mal y pense*—clearly
represents a philosophical judgment about other religions rather
than a genuine understanding of their specificity, let alone a valid
generalization from empirical data. Preaching this kind of universalism—the essential unity of the infinitely many ways to the
Infinite One—is itself a very specific and definite religious, viz.
philosophical, option. The Christians in India were quick to

perceive this when confronted with the danger of seeing this view adopted as an official ideology and taught in schools. Secularism was a good thing, or so at least the Indian Christians felt, as long as it gave scope to each religious group to be itself and to teach its doctrines without social, cultural and missionary interference from other (especially majority) groups. But to teach the unity or equal validity of all religions would constitute a missionary intrusion of the Gandhi or Radhakrishnan type of Hinduism into the autonomous sphere of Christianity.

The same problem is illustrated in an even more telling manner by the relation of modern Hinduism to Buddhism. Unlike Christianity which wanted to swallow up its parent religion Judaism (for in a *heilsgeschichtliche* perspective the dispensation of the Old Israel is superseded by, and integrated into, its fulfilment in the New Israel, the Church), Hinduism tries to swallow its heretical daughter religion. Far from being the great rebel (see above, p. 97) the Buddha, according to this view, was a Hindu reformer whose roots were in the Upanishads. What he called the *dharma* was really Upanishadic teaching.

The Buddha did not feel that he was announcing a new religion. He was born, grew up, and died a Hindu . . . Buddhism did not start as a new and independent religion . . . The Buddha utilized the Hindu inheritance to correct some of its expressions. He came to fulfil, not to destroy. For us, in this country, the Buddha is an outstanding representative of our religious tradition . . . While the teaching of the Buddha assumed distinctive forms in other countries of the world in conformity with their own traditions, here, in the home of the Buddha, it has entered into and become an integral part of our culture.

I have quoted from an address delivered by Radhakrishnan during the great Buddha Jayanti, celebrated also in India (1956) as a major state occasion. It can be safely left to the reader's imagination to guess the reactions of Buddhists (as well as of conservative Hindus) to Radhakrishnan's encomium. These reactions are of interest not only to the student of contemporary history and sociology but also to the comparative religionist, for they may help dispel the notion, so dear to scholars in the West and East alike, that Eastern religions are inclusive whereas Western religions are intolerantly exclusive. Even so sensitive a scholar as Wilfred C. Smith has chided the 'Western convention to talk of the religions of the world, imagining these as so many distinct entities, each a system of its own. Within such a framework, Westerners have learned to speak of three religions in China, and to label these Confucianist, Taoist, and Buddhist' (W. C. Smith 1963). The Chinese example is instructive because the ancient Chinese did have a syncretistic theory of the unity of the three religions. But the very development of the doctrine of *san-chiao* (Jap. *san-gyō*) provides the best possible evidence of the awareness of basic differences. In fact, the Chinese, like Westerners, were aware of the presence of three religions. It may be apposite here to remind ourselves of what the great Zen master Dōgen had to say on the subject, remembering at the same time that Dōgen Zenji was Japanese and not European or American, and hence when he spoke of *san-gyō* he did, indeed, refer to Taoism, Confucianism and Buddhism, and not to Catholics, Protestants and Jews, or to Jews, Christians and Muslims.

It is said that the essence of the three religions is identical . . . that the difference is only that of the entrance into the Way [and not of the Way itself], and also that they are comparable to the three legs of a tripod . . . This is the greatest folly. The phrase 'the identity of the three religions' is worse than the babble of babes . . . If people say such things, Buddhism has already gone from them.

But let us return to our main theme. The study of religion, whilst entertaining its own assumptions regarding the unity—not of religion or religions, but—of the anthropological and social structures underlying the phenomenon of religion is not committed to any philosophical view of the nature of religion. It must be stressed, however, once again that it has its own methodological and ideological presuppositions, and that these, no doubt, provide ample opportunity to the theologians to complain that the 'secular' study of religion distorts the self-understanding of the faith which it purports to study. Wishing to avoid getting bogged down in yet another discussion of the possibilities and nature of a phenomenology of religion, I have so far merely argued that the Marxist and Freudian analyses, far from explaining religion away, may help to deepen our understanding of the phenomenon. Symbolizing the realities of human and social experience, religion cannot be fully understood without a better understanding of the realities with which it symbolically deals— and alienation is one of them. The original context of Marx's dictum is far more moving and profound than the 'opium of the people' phrase—subsequently degraded to a cheap slogan— suggests when quoted out of context. This does not alter the fact that religion has often been an even cheaper and less serious commodity than opium. It has served as a sugar-coating. Much bourgeois religion was of this type, and students of social history need not be told that, especially in industrialized Europe, religion was the sugar-coating of the middle classes rather than the opium of the people: most of the proletariat was indifferent to religion which, however, maintained or even increased its hold on the bourgeoisie. Some non-bourgeois, but none the less typically middle-class phenomena of Hippie religion (including Zen without tears, Instant Enlightenment and guru worship) fall into the same category.

The somewhat culinary subtitle of this chapter has omitted one important food item that has served as a symbol as well as sacrament in religious history: the bread of life. The question is whether post-modern religion can still have this function. The secular dimensions of modernity have generated attitudes, structures, mental and motivational complexes, value orientations, and social and cultural patterns that possess their autonomous qualities. Religion, as a symbolic reference system, may set them within some framework of meaning. If so, religion can perhaps also act as a vitamin: it is no food at all, but it enables the body to assimilate food which must come from elsewhere, and to convert it into body-substance.

Will this function be taken over by new forms of religion, or is there room in the structure of modernity for tradition? Modernity, being the contemporary expression of social, i.e., human life, embodies in its own ways the basic conflicts and problems that also were the stuff of tradition. In the words of J. Heesterman (Heesterman 1973a), 'there hardly seems room for a conflict between tradition and modernity. For whatever room there is had already been taken up by the unresolved conflict of tradition itself. Modernity, then, would seem to find its predestined place within tradition's own, essentially broken and contradictory framework ... Tradition can only deal with the insoluble by being itself an unresolved conflict'. Consequently modernity, in fact anything 'alien' or 'novel', is often welcomed in changing and developing societies in addition to serving, in the Third World, the convenient function of precipitating the standard anti-Western reflexes. This is so because that which is modern can, by virtue of being alien, serve as a convenient peg on which to hang the awareness of conflict, contradiction and tension. Modernity can symbolize the lure of the new. Tradition, on the other hand, possesses its own characteristic patina: the deceptive appearance of integration and of the resolution of conflict. Hence it requires 'modern' elements to offer new ways of dealing with the long-standing, unresolved conflicts in tradition by reviving and exacerbating them. Tradition can serve as a mechanism of adaptation to modernity; it may also provide and determine what E. Shils (1971) has called the 'idiom of rejection'. Modernity brings its own dislocations, its alluring promises, its incompatibilities with tradition, and it generates in many instances the at times fruitful and at times paralysing conflicts of a partial and unintegrated realization of modernity. But at the same time, in doing so, it also responds to the inner conflicts present in our existence, i.e., in all culture and hence also in all tradition. Hence:

successful modernity does not mean the suppression of tradition or the superimposition on it of a different order. It means that the inner conflict of tradition is now fought within the confines of an expanded reality . . . Authority and legitimation are no longer transcendent and safe in an ultramundane sphere but part of reality—and therefore constantly called into question. In contradistinction to tradition, modernity must valorize change because the authority of its code . . . no longer transcends reality. Modernity has not solved the inner conflict of tradition, nor can it ever do so. But it has fundamentally changed it by carrying it over into the sphere of a single explosive reality.

At the confines of that reality man still encounters the enigma of transcendence, and it is there that he constructs his system of meanings. Does this imply that religion will always exist? Martin Buber used to say that all religions were *essentially* different, but that in the end of days all would pass away in the fullness of the Kingdom of God. Buber could formulate this, his version of an eschatological myth, because as an anti-Platonist, he did not believe in essences. For Buber, if I may say so, the essence was not really essential. And having quoted, in this chapter, both Dōgen Zenji and Martin Buber, I would conclude with a story that brings the two together in Jerusalem and which I heard from one of our generation's great Zen masters. It is the story of a fruitful misunderstanding, and of an encounter in which one participant did all the talking, the second participant did all the listening, and the third participant did nothing at all.

The Zen master was invited on a tour around the world by an ardent American admirer. When the two came to Jerusalem they called on Buber. The American talked, Buber listened, and the Zen master sat in silence. With great verve the American held forth that all religions were basically one, different variations on an identical theme, manifold manifestations of one and the same essence. Buber gave him one of his long, piercing looks, and then shot at him the question: 'And what is the essence?' At this point the Zen master could not contain himself: he jumped from his seat and with both hands shook the hands of Buber.

NOTES

pp. 1–3. The basic problems and issues related to religion in the modern age are discussed in most textbooks of sociology of religion. Many of the more recent ones already contain critical discussions of the theses and theories advanced not only by the 'classical' authors but also by contemporary writers. I have found Savramis (1968), R. Robertson (1970; especially chapters 7 and 8), Scharf (1970; especially chapters 4, 7, and 8) and Matthes (1967) particularly helpful. Scharf already contains a good discussion of the theories of Berger, Luckmann, Wilson (1966), MacIntyre (1967) and others. Matthes (1967) is not a book of readings—like Birnbaum and Lenzer (1969)—but one of the best introductions and a major contribution to the sociology of religion, especially with regard to the problem of secularization; the appended anthology of readings also includes more recent authors (Schelsky, T. Rendtorff *et al.*). The great classics are discussed in Glock and Hammond (1973). As regards definitions of religion, one of the most thoughtful recent contributions is that of Bianchi (1972). Since there is constant interaction between the more theoretical attempts at definition and the actual *praxis* of historians of religion, attention should also be drawn to the valuable essays of Puech (1970) and especially Brelich (1970).

There are few overall surveys of contemporary religious developments, though there are many detailed studies of individual religions, areas and groups. Some useful, though in some respects slightly out of date, accounts can be found in Kitagawa (1959).

'Disenchantment' (p. 3) is the usual English translation of Max Weber's *Entzauberung*, though the alternative rendering 'de-mystification' has much to recommend it.

pp. 3–8. The ways in which the Western origins of modernity and modernization affect the cultural as well as emotional responses of other civilizations are touched upon in subsequent chapters, and hence no detailed references are given here. On the re-evaluation and re-examination of Weber, see Nelson (1973) and Eisenstadt (1973b).

pp. 8–12. The reference to the 'poverty of historicism' should not be construed as a polemical jibe against Popper (1960). Unfortunately there is no good English equivalent to the distinction, made by German writers, between *Historismus* and *Historizismus*. The good bibliography on 'historicism' at the end of the encyclopaedia article by Mandelbaum (1967) relieves me of the necessity of listing here the relevant works of Troeltsch, Meinecke, Dilthey, Croce *et al.* The description of the death-of-god celebration as a pop-style 'happening' I owe to Hartmann (1969) quoting H. J. Schultz. On the subject of secularization the most significant contributions are in German: Lübbe (1965); Blumenberg (1966); Matthes (1967); Kamlah (1969). Mention should also be made of the work of Nijk (1968). Wilson (1966) and MacIntyre (1967) have already been mentioned, and Martin (1969) is referred to in the main text. Of course all modern studies of religion deal, either explicitly or by implication, with secularization. The use of the term in modern theology is discussed in the next chapter. For sociologists who emphasize the element of continuity in the 'secularized' transformations of originally non-secular values, much of the modern sociology of culture becomes a sociology of 'items of secularization' (*Säkularisate*).

pp. 12–14. The most recent major study of modernization is that of Eisenstadt (1973c) with full bibliography; cf. also Eisenstadt (1968). For non-European societies see also Eisenstadt (1973b); Geertz (1963); Bellah (1965); D. E. Smith (1974) and the various works and articles referred to throughout this book. Among the various terms invented to bridge the gap between 'traditional' and 'modern' is that much-worked but useful horse 'post-traditional'; cf. the issue devoted to the subject by *Daedalus* (1973).

pp. 14–16. A random sample may illustrate to what extent this terminology is 'in' at present and the problem which it reflects is a central concern: Edwards (1969); Eisenstadt (1973a); Gellner (1964); M. Mead, *Continuities in Cultural Evolution* (1964); F. M. Deng, *Tradition and Modernization: A Challenge for Law among the Dinka of the Sudan* (1971); J. K. Fairbank, E. O. Reischauer and M. A. Craig (eds.), *East Asia: Tradition and Transformation* (1973). Prof. J. Gonda entitled a collection of his articles and papers *Change and Continuity in Indian Religion* (1965), and M. Singer and B. S. Cohen edited a volume of studies on India under the title *Structure and Change in Indian Society* (1968). The Proceedings of the Second Conference on Shinto Studies organized at Kokugakuin University in Tokyo appeared as *Continuity and Change in Shinto* (1967). Variations on these themes will be found in many of the titles quoted or referred to in subsequent chapters. Also symposia and collective volumes increasingly tend to exhibit these terms; cf., e.g., vol. vii of the *International Yearbook for the Sociology of Religion* devoted to 'Religion and Social Change' (1971) or the volume *Probleme des Kulturwandels im 20. Jahrhundert* (1965), published by the 'Forschungsstelle für Weltzivilisation'. 'Religion and Cultural Change' was also the subject of the final chapter of Christopher Dawson's 1947 Gifford Lectures (Dawson, 1948). Dawson sees religion as a unifying force in times of cultural synthesis, and as a revolutionary force in times of cultural disintegration. He is aware of the basic instability of the relation between the two: if religion is too deeply committed to a particular cultural synthesis, it fails to maintain its transcendent character; if it attempts to emancipate itself completely from its bond with culture, it makes for the secularization of the latter. Dawson's interesting, though conservative and somewhat biased study can also serve as an illustration of the changes in the styles of sociological thinking.

pp. 16–17. There is a vast literature discussing the propriety or impropriety of making an absolute contrast of the pair Tradition-Modernity. See, e.g., Shils (1971); Kothari (1968); Bendix (1966–7); Gusfield (1966–7), and the numerous publications of Milton Singer on India. Cf. also Eisenstadt (1973a) and the remarkable study of India by Rudolph and Rudolph, *The Modernity of Tradition* (1967). In one way or another the subject is touched upon in almost every one of the studies cited in this book. Cf. also the very thoughtful essay by Pieper (1974).

pp. 18–20. Formations with 'post-' are a favourite neologism nowadays. Post-modern, like post-traditional, is already well established. D. Bell has familiarized us with *The Coming of Post-Industrial Society* (1973)—the term itself being pre-Bell. Some sociologists have even spoken of 'post-peasants' (Weingrod and Morin, in *Comparative Studies in Society and History* vol. 13, 1971). Theologians speak as a matter of course of our 'post-religious age' (e.g., Novak 1965, pp. 35–44), and it is by now a commonplace that modern man is a 'post-historic man'—whatever that may mean (cf., e.g., Seidenberg, 1960). The term *Posthistoire*, coined by earlier writers, has been taken up recently by A. Gehlen in a thoughtful essay (Gehlen 1974); see also O. Köhler, 'Die Zeit der Nachgeschichte' (Köhler 1965), and Wheelis (1971).

As for 'Beyond', the list could be infinitely extended; one thinks of L. Trilling's *Beyond Culture* (1955) and B. F. Skinner's *Beyond Freedom and Dignity* (1972). The collection of sociological studies *Beyond the Classics?* (Hammond and Glock 1973) has already been mentioned. The title of Bellah (1970) combines 'beyond' and 'post-traditional'. Milton Singer's 'Beyond Tradition and Modernity in Madras' originally appeared in *Comparative Studies in Society and History* vol. 13 (1971), pp. 160–95.

The mention of Durkheim's name (p. 19) provides me with an occasion for stating very emphatically my belief in the continued relevance and fruitfulness of the insights of this great pioneer. This homage is necessary because Durkheim is mentioned much less than Weber in the pages of this book, and occasionally he is mentioned with an undertone of criticism. The continued relevance of Durkheim is brought out by many recent studies, e.g., König (1961, 1962); Parsons (1973); Bellah (1973).

CHAPTER II

pp. 21–3. The 'indigenization' of the African churches in particular is an extremely fascinating phenomenon because it takes place on two distinct levels: the 'separatist' native movements, churches and sects on the one hand, and the policies adopted by 'establishment' bodies such as the Roman Catholic

e.g., the almost interminable series *Kerygma und Mythos*; Robinson and Edwards
(1963); Ice and Carey (1967). One of the best surveys of the subject in English
is Sperna Weiland (1968). For the sake of completeness the three main surveys
by Sperna Weiland (in Dutch) should be mentioned here: *Oriëntatie* (1966,
5th impression 1971, with chapters on Tillich, Bultmann, Bonhoeffer, Robinson,
P. van Buren, H. Cox, W. Hamilton, Th. Altizer, D. Sölle and others);
Voortgezette Oriëntatie (2nd enlarged ed. 1971, with chapters on E. Bloch, H.
Marcuse, neo-Marxism, D. Sölle, J. Moltmann, J. B. Metz, political theology
etc.); *Het Einde van de Religie* (1970, subtitled 'Following the trail of Bonhoeffer'.)
Of the many critical discussions of the new theology I found C. Duquoc (1972)
and *Mise en Question 1* (1970) among the best. Cf. also the article by Torrance
cited by Martin (1969), p. 75, n. 1. Zahrnt (1970) is one of the most serious
and thoughtful discussions in German of the death-of-God theology. Hartmann
(1969) too is very valuable and helpful. Mention must also be made of W. C.
Smith (1967).

The relations of modern theology and Marxism present too weighty a
subject to be dealt with in a note, especially as the spectrum is very wide and
ranges from theological flirtation to theological *cache-misère*. Some Christian
'syntheses' are extremely naïve (e.g., Gonzales-Ruis, 1971), whilst certain
attempts at dialogue have been very thorough and tough-minded. It must
suffice here to refer to the dialogue in France with Roger Garaudy as the
(then) official Communist spokesman; to Gollwitzer (1970; the original
German edition appeared in 1962 in the series *Marxismusstudien*); and to
Desroche (1962). Cf. also José Maria Diez-Alegría's *I Believe in Hope* (1973)
with its message 'I believe in Jesus Christ . . . I am indebted to Karl Marx'.
It is unnecessary to emphasize that it is the spirit of E. Bloch that is hovering
over the waters of the new political theology. References to Buddhist-Marxist
contacts will be found in chapter V, but I would emphasize here the significant
fact that serious religious encounters with Marxism (as distinct from naïve
use of catch-phrases) in Asia take place under Christian auspices. A recent
good example is the Marxist-Christian-Buddhist encounter held 4–6 May
1974 at the dialogue centre of the Jesuit fathers in Kandy, Sri Lanka (Ceylon).
See also Ling (1966).

For Latin American theology cf., e.g., Gutierrez (1972; the original ed.
appeared in Lima in 1971 as *Teologia de la liberación*). The role of Marxism
in Latin American Catholicism is not really a matter of Christian theology
but a function of the sociological structure of Latin American countries and
of the range of elites, intellectuals, non-intellectual or semi-intellectual potential
bearers of protest and contestation, as well as of the 'idioms of protest' available
in the Latin American situation. On the whole subject cf. Houtart and Pin
(1965); Houtart and Rousseau (1971; cf. also the French version 1972); Sanders
(1974); as well as the contributions of D. E. Smith, Behrman, Kantor and
Grayson in D. E. Smith, ed. (1974).

Church or the World Council of Churches (viz. the churches
the latter) on the other.

Some of the best discussions of the semantic as well as cultu
'secularization' can be found in the German works mentioned
to chapter I (supra, p. 117). Kamlah (1969) also makes interestin
for distinguishing between secularization, profanization, etc. Th
secularization is discussed under the heading 'de-sacralization'—a
cent of one of the major concerns of Mircea Eliade's work—in B
Valuable, though debatable, insights into the nature of the E
will be found in Horkheimer and Adorno (1972, the original Ge
appeared in 1947).

pp. 23–5. Troeltsch's essay, which appeared in 1909, w
delivered as a lecture in 1901. There is sound sociological metho
the progression of Matthes' *Religionssoziologie* (Matthes 1967) in
Kirchensoziologie (Matthes 1969) in vol. 2. On the same problem
remarkable essay of Rendtorff (1966). A major study of *kyō–han*
expected from the pen of Prof. I. H. Kamstra of the University of .

pp. 26–8. As regards the 'functionalist' appraisal of religion, cf.
of T. S. Eliot (1939, p.58): 'And what is worst of all is to advocate
not because it is true, but because it might be beneficial'. The
contemporary form of the loss of religion has also been noted by I
Murray (1964) who distinguishes between the 'old modern' and
modern' problem. The latter is said to lie 'in the historical-existentia.
not in the purely cognitive one. The expression 'modernization o
occurs on p. ix of Bellah's Introduction to Bellah, 1965. On the wh
see also the valuable and interesting symposium volume edited by C
Grumelli (1971).

pp. 28–30. The classical manifesto of the theology of secularity is
(1953), well analysed by Kamlah (1963), pp. 58 ff. Since then ther
an unending series of at times more, at times less, sophisticated t
somersaults. An interesting phenomenological comparison could
between Protestant and Catholic versions of this theology, the la
trying to combine the notion of secularity with that of sacrament;
the title of a recent Roman Catholic encyclopaedia *Sacramentum Mur*
by Karl Rahner (1968–70), or the definition offered by Panikkar (1
me secularization represents the regaining of the sacramental str
reality' (p. 92). It may be appropriate at this point to remind oursel
objections raised against Bultmann by most of his critics: the real iss
de-mythologization is not myth as such, but the fact that many of
myths have become meaningless and that modern man, and espec
modern theologian, is in quest of new myths.

The various contributions to the new theology have produced a
'debates' which, in their turn, have produced a stream of secondary li

I

pp. 30–2. The view that, in spite of their modern and non-clerical appearances, the new radical theologies of secularization simply 'continue the old imperialism of the Church with other means' is also argued by Nijk (1968) who suggests that 'secularization' is frequently 'a kind of cultural house arrest which contemporary theologians impose on their fellow-men'. Nijk also points out the element of 'artful apologetic' hidden under the veneer of radical theology. As a random sample of modern Christian theologies chasing each other to catch up with the latest fashion, the following may serve: Sölle (1971); Gutierrez (1972); Moltmann (1967, 1969, 1972, 1973); Cobb (1972); Daly (1973). Strictly speaking Daly's work is anti-Christian and hence somewhat out of context here. Rosemary Ruether might be a better example of an *engagée* Christian theologian of liberation (including feminism). But Daly's feminist paroxysms are so much geared to the Christian tradition that her anti-theology is best viewed by the historian under the general heading of 'Christianity'.

Cox's recent encomium to the new quest for self-realization, self-fulfilment, etc., is another example of the ability to keep the fingers on the pulse of the *Zeitgeist*. Disillusioned former militants as well as former drug-experimenters in the U.S. seem to be passing through a period of passive opposition to technology, science, achievement norms and other features of the 'Western tradition'. For all this, Eastern Wisdom (or Perennial, viz. Ancient Wisdom which is, of course, located in the East) serves as a convenient 'idiom of rejection'; see Pope (1974). Pending the publication of the Bay Area Study under the direction of Bellah and Glock, see also I. Needleman (1970), Marvin H. Harper (1972), and Robert S. Ellwood (1973) for the American scene.

pp. 33–4. An interesting Catholic history of modern atheism, especially of the theologies of atheism and its precursors and successors, is given by Fabro (1968); the work originally appeared in Italian under the title *Introduzione all'Ateismo Moderno* (1964). Lacroix (1958) has been translated into English under the title *The Meaning of Modern Atheism* (1965) with a preface by Fr. Garret Barden s.j. The literature on modern atheism and around the question whether it is a 'religious' or 'irreligious' phenomenon, is immense. Cf. Marty (1964); Fr. Martin D'Arcy (1962); Heer and Szczesny (1962); Novak (1965). The projected second volume of the series *Mise en Question* is to be entitled *Le Christianisme à l'épreuve de l'athéisme*. Sartre's claims to carry on his shoulders the burden of heroic atheism can be found, e.g. in *L'existentialisme est un humanisme* (1946) and again, more recently, in *Les Mots* (1965). An interesting attempt at an analysis of unbelief—unfortunately marred by apologetic tendencies—was undertaken by Rümke (1952).

What has been called here the 'new gospel of shrinkage in the direction of secular-activity-in-the-world' may well be an understatement. Whilst many of the political demonstrations and resolutions of, e.g., the *World Council of Churches*, exhibit a great deal of naïveté, self-righteousness, hypocrisy and uncritical capitulation to fashionable slogans, there is at least the attempt to act out of a genuinely Christian commitment. In other cases the Christian element has been reduced to zero and one wonders why the Christian cloak is still wrapped around political leftism. A good example is provided by the literature put out by the *Evangelische Studentengemeinde* (ESG) in Germany; cf. the remarks of Prof. M. Thielicke in the *Deutsche Zeitung* of 25 January 1974. Some of the 'shrinkage' is also discernible in Latin America. To be avant-garde means that the Christology of Chalcedon and the traditions deriving from it have become irrelevant or positively to be rejected. Jesus is either a revolutionary prototype of Ché Guevara and Camillo Torres, or the representative of the anonymous poor and the 'marginal' victims of society.

pp. 35–9. As regards religionless Christianity (see Jenkins 1962; also Sperna Weiland 1970) it should be pointed out here that there are various strategies of salvaging a religionless religion from the wreckage wrought by the radical theologies. One of them is to consider 'theology' and not 'religion' to be the villain: theology falsifies the true nature of religion. This is the line taken also by Ling (1966). Alternatively one makes a distinction between 'religion' (institutionalized, externalized and objectified—and hence negative) on the one hand, and 'belief' or 'faith' on the other. Of course, further distinctions can be made between 'belief' and 'faith', reminiscent of (though very different from) the classical distinction between *fides quae creditur* and *fides qua creditur*. Cf. Pieper (1963), and the section entitled *Clarifications: Belief and Faith* in Novak (1965). For the criticism of radical theology as a disguised bourgeois ideology see *Mise en Question I* (1970). The making-a-virtue-of-necessity quality of much modern theology of secularization is also pointed out by Nijk (1968).

CHAPTER III

pp. 40–2. Some of the paragraphs in this chapter (as well as in some other chapters), especially those dealing with universalism and particularity, are lifted *verbatim* from Werblowsky (1971). On the relation of pluralism and secularization, see Berger (1967), Yinger (1967), and Glock's comments on Yinger (ibid., pp. 28–30). The literature on pluralism has increased steadily since H. R. Niebuhr's classic (Niebuhr, H. Richard, 1929). It is enough to mention the names of, e.g., Martin E. Marty, Franklin H. Littell and W. Herberg even without listing their writings. Special mention should, however, be made of Herberg (1955). On the emergence of modern Jewry from the ghetto see Katz (1973). The various aspects of the struggle for emancipation, assimilation, re-formulation of cultural, social and national identity, national revival and Zionism are discussed in practically every historical or sociological study of modern Judaism as well as of modern anti-semitism (cf., e.g., Tal 1971a). The question whether modern developments do not spell the end of the Jewish people is raised by Friedmann (1968, the original French version appeared in 1965); the same problem is discussed, albeit from a very different angle, by E. Simon (1949; 1953). The expression *communitas communitarum* is borrowed from Buber (1958).

pp. 43–4. The T. S. Eliot quotation is taken from Eliot (1934), p. 20. There is also much in Eliot (1939) and Eliot (1948) that should be of interest to readers of this book. The effect of American denominational pluralism on the Jewry and Judaism of the U.S. has been discussed in innumerable books and articles since Herberg's pioneer study. On the ideology of Zionism see Hertzberg (1969) and Katz (1971); the latter essay also brings out the 'messianic' elements present in the modern national movement.

pp. 45–8. A philosophical account of the history of modern Jewish thought and thinkers is given by Rotenstreich (1968, 1972). Examples of contemporary theological and para-theological efforts are Bokser (1957); Cohen (1962); Gordis (1955); Herberg (1951); Sleeper and Mintz (1971); Wolf (1965). See also the writings listed in Borowitz (1970). Impressive and penetrating reflections on the present situation of Jewish theology have recently been presented by Scholem (1974). The most serious thinker on the subject of the Holocaust is Fackenheim (1970, 1972). The approach of the historian rather than the philosopher is exemplified by Ben-Sasson (1971).

pp. 48–53. On the interaction of religion and politics in Israel see E. Goldman (1964), and—although inadequate—Seliger (1968) and Zucker (1974). The expression 'conversion to the world' is borrowed from the title of Schultz (1964). The Eddington quotation is from his Swarthmore Lecture (Eddington 1929).

pp. 54–5. Rosenzweig's *Stern*, though not published until 1921, was written in the trenches during World War I on little scraps of paper. This is not the place to enquire whether, and to what extent, Rosenzweig modified some of his views in his later writings. The term 'eclipse' of God (used also *supra*, p. 46) is taken from the title of one of Buber's best-known books (actually the title of its first essay); see Buber (1952).

pp. 56–7. My account of Kook's theology of secularity is heavily indebted to Schweid (1969). One of the most stimulating and provocative contributions to the discussion of Zionism and secular Judaism is J. Bloch (1971). An interesting example of an 'idiom of rejection' was provided by the short-lived 'Canaanite' movement in Israel; see Kurzweil (1953).

pp. 57–60. Since this chapter does not discuss Japanese religion as such, no bibliography on the subject is required. It should be noted, however, that whilst the literature on modernization is immense, that on religion and secularization is disappointingly poor. Historians and sociologists of religion seem to prefer studying the so-called 'New Religions' or sects rather than the greater and more basic problem of secularization; cf., e.g., Morioka (1969). For change in Shinto see the Proceedings of the Second Conference on Shinto

Studies (Kokugakuin 1967). Sh. Ueda (1971) has many interesting things to say, but his account falls between two stools since it deals neither with Buddhism (but only with Japan) nor with Japan (since Buddhism is only one segment of the Japanese religious and cultural spectrum). Valuable insights are contained in C. Blacker's unpublished MS 'Sacred and Secular in Japanese Religion'. The universalist potential in Shinto is asserted by Kenji Ueda (1972), p. 45. For the revaluation of 'traditional' (the current euphemism for 'primitive') religions as part of contemporary national and cultural revitalization tendencies also by Christian theologians; cf., e.g., E. Bolaji Idowu (1973).

CHAPTER IV

pp. 61–4. There is a vast literature on the problems generated for Islam by the encounter with the West and with modernity generally, and on Islamic 'modernism' in particular. Most of the books and articles cited or referred to in this chapter contain bibliographies that can serve as guides for further reading. A brief general survey is given in chapter 10 of Gibb (1970, all quotations are from this edition. The first edition of the book appeared in 1949.) Special mention should be made of Rahman (1966), chapters 12–14; see also Rahman (1955, 1970, 1974). The major study on the subject is W. C. Smith (1957), and it is much to be regretted that the author has not taken time off from his subsequent work to produce a second edition carrying his account forward to the early seventies. Cf. also Gibb (1932); Gibb (1947); Grunebaum (1962); to which should be added specific as well as comparative studies of modern Islam in specific areas, e.g., Adams (1933); Adams (1959); W. C. Smith (1951); A. Ahmad (1967a, 1967b); and Geertz (1968)—one of the most outstanding contributions not only to the study of Islam but also to that of religion in general. On the subject of Islamic 'decline' or 'decadence' see also the titles listed in Turner (1974), p. 243, n. 37.

The paradox of Islam as an individual-eschatological message turning into a societal or even political religion is compounded by the fact that the Prophet (unlike, e.g., the Old Testament) never enunciated a definite social or political theory. Some of the historical problems as well as possibilities of Islam may be connected with this fact, and 'it is perhaps not just accidental that the Prophet left no instructions as to the community's form of government' (Heesterman 1973a, p. 113, n. 29).

pp. 65–9. For a random sample of modern Christian theologies proclaiming the gospel of the latest intellectual fashion, cf. supra in the notes to chapter 2, p. 121. For the example of social apologetic in connection with *zakat*, cf. Nieuwenhuijze (1958), p. 208. For the casuistic-legalistic, i.e. traditionalist, procedures of the *'ulama* in 'solving' modern problems, cf. Lazarus-Yafeh (1971). See also the other contributions to the same volume (Baer 1971). A good example of apologetic modernism (e.g. on the subject of monogamy) is Ameer Ali (1922).

pp. 69–73. On scripturalism in general and 'scripturalist nationalism' in particular (e.g., Al-Fassi's National Action Movement in North Africa) see Geertz; cf. also the case study of Gellner (1963). On the remarkable case of the Murids see O'Brien (1970) and Gellner (1973). For the problem of *Wirtschaftsethik* and Islam, see most recently Turner (1974) and the literature cited there. On Islamic socialism see the excellent essay of Rahman (1974) as well as the chapters by Crecelius, Minault, and G. Lewy in the same volume (D. E. Smith 1974); see also below, pp. 78–9. For modern commentaries on the Qur'an see Baljon (1961).

pp. 73–80. Many of the studies referred to in the foregoing contain discussions of, and bibliographies on, Islam and modern nationalism. It is in the nature of things that some of the more important studies on the subject (and of nationalism in Asia and Africa generally, as well as its relation to socialism) were made not by historians of religion but by political scientists. On Muslim reactions to the West see Gibb (1962) chapter 14, and Lewis (1964); cf. also Frye (1957). On the paradox of anti-Western ideology as the ambiguous bequest of the West to the Third World, cf. the sobering assessment of Kedourie (1968), p. 464: 'Resentment and impatience, the depravity of the rich and the virtue of the poor, the guilt of Europe and the innocence of Asia and Africa, salvation through violence, the coming reign of universal love: these are the elements of the thought of Sultan Galiyev and Li Ta-chao, of Ikki Kita, Michel Aflaq, and Frantz Fanon. This theory is now the most popular and influential one in Asia and Africa. It is Europe's latest gift to the world. As Karl Marx remarked, theory itself becomes a material force when it has seized the masses; and with the printing-press, the transistor and television—those other gifts of Europe— it is easy now for theory, any theory, to seize the masses. Theory has become the opium of the masses. Marx, however, was wrong in thinking opium a mere soporific. As the Old Man of the Mountain—whose "theory" was so potent that legend has transmuted it into *hashish*—could have told him, the drug may also excite its addicts to a frenzy of destruction.'

An interesting and stimulating, though not always convincing thesis relating some of Islam's problems of modernization to certain structural aspects of the Arab language is argued by Freund (1971).

For most of the material on anti-Islamic, anti-religious radicalism I am indebted to conversations with my colleague Professor Y. Harkabi. It is greatly to be hoped that Professor Harkabi will find the time to write up and publish the large and fascinating amount of material which he has assembled. Meanwhile I am greatly in his debt for permitting me to make use of some of his material (e.g., concerning Al-Bitar, Al-Azm, Adonis) in the account presented on pp. 73, 76–7, and 80. Cf. however the observation of Rahman (1974, p. 243, n. 1): 'Muslim Marxists do not abandon Islam, at least openly'. The classic discussion of Islam from a Marxist point of view still is Rodinson (1966); see also Rodinson (1972). On the problem of Islam and secularism see Gallagher (1966).

pp. 81–2. See also the chapter on Islam in W. C. Smith (1963). The use of the term *Stellvertretung* is meant as a direct reference to the 'radical theology' type of Christology offered by D. Sölle, *Stellvertretung: ein Kapitel Theologie nach dem 'Tode Gottes'* (1965).

CHAPTER V

pp. 83–8. One of the more recent defences of the title of 'religion' for Buddhism is Ling (1966); cf. also Glasenapp (1970, the original German version appeared in 1954 as *Buddhismus und Gottesidee*, subsequently re-edited in 1966 by H. Bechert with a selection of Buddhist texts under the title *Der Buddhismus: eine atheistische Religion*). The analysis of this-worldly *versus* other-worldly orientations is a standard feature of all discussions of religion since Weber. The literature on modern change in India is immense, and among the most important contributions to our understanding of modern Hinduism are those made by social scientists; cf., e.g., the works of Srinivas, Singer, D. E. Smith and Heesterman listed in the bibliography, as well as the volumes of *Contributions to Indian Sociology*. See also the chapters dealing with India in D. E. Smith (1974). One of the best accounts of modern Hinduism is Gonda (1963), pp. 253–345, with ample bibliography. The great classic on caste (as well as on many other features of Indian civilization and religion) is Dumont 1970 (the original French version appeared in 1966; much of the material had been published previously in *Contributions to Indian Sociology*); cf. also the Review Symposium 'On the Nature of Caste in India', devoted to Dumont's work and published in *Contributions to Indian Sociology* N.S. vol. 5 (1971). The quotation (p. 85) from W. Temple is from *Nature, Man and God*, 1949, p. 36.

The relationship between Hindu renewal and Indian nationalism is discussed in practically all works dealing with modern Indian history. Social and political scientists rightly give much attention to the relationship of "communalism" and religion (e.g., Dumont, op. cit.). The significance of nationalism as well as of the Western influences is nicely brought out by the title of Gonda's chapter (1963) on modern Hinduism: part 1 'Die Praxis des neueren Hinduismus'; part 2: 'Religiöse und weltanschauliche Strömungen unter der Einwirkung des Abendlandes, der religiöse Nationalismus und die Renaissance des Hinduismus'.

On the subject of 'holy cows' see Margul (1968) and the slightly sarcastic but sobering account in Schmid (1961), pp. 51–7. His chapter on 'Cows— Sacred Sufferers' also gives examples of modern Hindu rationalizations (pp. 52–3). Of course, none of the bizarre modern rationalizations (e.g., the cow representing the mother that nourishes us with her milk) will explain why a pious Hindu stands a better chance of safely crossing the river Vaitarani (the Hindu equivalent of the underworld river Styx) if he holds a cow's tail in his hand at the moment of death; cf. also Glasenapp (1922), pp. 67–9.

pp. 88–91. On Kautilya and the Arthashastra see Heesterman (1971a) and also his remarks (1973a); also D. E. Smith (1963), pp. 59–61. On ancient Indian political thought see also Basham (1964). My treatment of Brahmanism and *sanyasa* is much indebted to Heesterman (1964, 1971b). It is almost superfluous to refer once again to the work of Louis Dumont. On the subject of house-holder and renouncer see also the judicious remarks of O'Flaherty (1973), pp. 78 f. On Tilak and the Ganpati festival see Barnouw (1954). The term 'sanskritization' was first introduced by Srinivas (1952); since then it (viz. its successor 'brahminization') has become a major conceptual tool in Indian studies. On the relationship of caste to processes of change and modernization see, e.g., Srinivas (1962, 1968); Singer and Cohn (1968), especially parts III and IV. The most recent *magnum opus* on the relation of Indian religion and modernization is Singer (1972). See also Singer's contribution to the aforementioned Review Symposium on Dumont, entitled 'Modernization or Traditionalization?'

pp. 92–3. Buddhist studies happen to be in a uniquely fortunate position as the result of the availability of the accumulated results of different types of research. The impressive results of the classical methods of historico-philological scholarship can now be supplemented by work bearing on social and political theory and history, as well as by intensive anthropological field-work. Thus we have the work of E. Michael Mendelson and M. Spiro (e.g., Spiro 1967, 1970) in Burma; of Tambiah (1968, 1970, 1973) in Thailand; of Obeyesekere, Yalman (1967) and Gombrich (1971) in Ceylon. Cf. also Fürer-Haimendorf (1967), Nash (1966), and Leach (1973). The bibliography which fills vol. iii (1973) of Bechert (1966–73) is complete and exhaustive. The bibliography in Sarkisyanz (1965) is, in the nature of things, more focussed on Burma; cf. also part 2 of Sarkisyanz (1955). A distinction partly similar to that quoted from Spiro (1970) can also be found in King (1964). The standard work on the Ashokan edicts is J. Bloch (1955), though Hultzsch (1925) is still indispensable. The phrases (p. 13) 'precept and practice' and 'dialectic of practical religion' are meant, needless to say, as indirect references to Gombrich (1971) and Leach (1968).

pp. 93–5. For the recommendation that an aspirant to arhatship should not do any good deeds see Obeyesekere (1968), p. 19, who quotes this 'famous statement' of the Buddha without indicating a source. The nearest canonical equivalent is verse 7 of the Padhâsutta (*Sutta-Nipata*, verse 430) in the Mahavagga; see Fausböll's translation in S.B.E. vol. x, part II (1891). My references to Cochrane's autobiography are taken from Sarkisyanz (1965), pp. 112–13. As regards Christian criticisms of Buddhism, cf. also the quotation from W. Temple, supra, p. 85. There exist more discussions of Buddhism by Christian theologians (including H. de Lubac) than can be listed here.

Weber's expression *Domestikationsmittel* can be found in *Gesammelte Aufsätze zur Religionssoziologie*, vol. 2 (1921), p. 265. For an older account, see Carus (1897).

pp. 95–9. Full documentation on the apologetic literature asserting the 'scientific' character of Buddhism will be found in Sarkisyanz and Bechert. Cf. also the statement of A. David [-Neel] (1911), p. 2., to the effect that Buddhism was 'proche des conclusions de la science d'aujourd'hui et, j'oserai dire, de la science de demain' as well as 'adéquat à la mentalité moderne'. For the relation of Buddhism to political action as well as to modern nationalisms, see—in addition to Bechert and Sarkisyanz—Mehden (1961); Shecter (1967); Swearer (1970, chapters 2 and 3). Readers who have no German and thus cannot profit from Bechert's *magnum opus* may consult his shorter English essays (Bechert 1969/70, 1973, 1974). On 'Buddhism and Political Power' see also King (1962b). The large literature on Buddhism and Marxism is discussed and listed by Sarkisyanz and Bechert; for an earlier account, cf. Trager (1959). See also Ling (1966), whose over-optimistic view of the future of Buddhism in China has to be reconsidered in the light of more recent accounts (Bush 1970; MacInnis 1972; Welch 1972).

Malalasekera (1973) was originally published in the *Buddhist World*; as the latter publication is inaccessible to me at the time of writing, I am quoting from a Malaysian reprint. The assertion made in that article to the effect that Buddhism 'seeks the meaning of life in life itself' already occurs in the title of an earlier essay by Malalasekera (1958/9). On the essentially conservative character of the Buddha's attitudes see also Bechert (1960/73), vol. i, pp. 7–8.

Those who share the writer's scepticism regarding the possibility of valid statements about the pre-Ashokan 'historical' Buddha will be puzzled and perplexed by the approach and method adopted by Ling (1973). It should be added, however, in all fairness, that a number of scholars reject much of the current historical (viz. methodological) scepticism as excessive; cf., e.g., Frauwallner (1957). My own evaluation of *The Revolt in the Temple* is identical to Bechert's (1966/73), vol. i, p. 41, n. 80), *contra* Benz (1963, p. 117). On the question whether or not laymen are full members of, viz. belong to, the Buddhist 'church', see Bechert, loc. cit., p. 67.

CHAPTER VI

p. 101. The title of the chapter and the imagery used in its first paragraph are, of course, drawn from *The Hunting of the Snark*. Nevertheless, even readers unfamiliar with Lewis Carroll's poem should be able to follow the argument of the chapter. A good example of a strictly empirical and quantitative sociological approach to the question of the future of religion will be found in the concluding chapters by Stark and Glock, and by Ch. Y. Glock, in Glock (1973a). The contributors to the symposium volume edited by Schatz (1971)

—including Berger and Luckmann—exhibit a different style of sociological analysis and seem to be more optimistic for the future of religion; cf. also Schatz (1974), especially the interesting contribution by Lübbe (1974). See also Szcesny (1965).

pp. 104–5. The distinction between religions in the plural (i.e., the historical phenomena known as such) and religion (with or without capital R) in the singular loses much of its force as our discussion turns to the future. This is in large measure due to the fact that as a result of cultural development in our shrinking world of rapid travel and communication, as well as of the 'fall-out' from the comparative study of religions (history, sociology, psychology, phenomenology of religion), religions impinge on one another, face one another and take one another seriously in new and significant ways. This phenomenon of convergence cannot be exorcized by an invocation of the spectre of 'syncretism'. Quite apart from the fact that one man's syncretism is another man's ecumenicism, one has to take into account that the nature of syncretisms too is subject to developments and changes. It certainly is not a matter of 'religions' joining forces against the enemy forces of materialism and atheism (since the contrast has become meaningless in the religious sensibility of many), but rather of the sense of a common responsibility for elucidating and preserving whatever dimensions of religiosity and/or spirituality attach to the human condition. The recent literature on the subject produced by theologians, philosophers and historians (including A. Toynbee) is vast, and the matter will be touched on again below (pp. 109 f.) in connection with *theologia religionum*. See also Lanczkowski (1971), and the chapter 'Religion ausserhalb der Religionen?' in Schlette (1971).

The ritual and cultic forms developing, and often manufactured, in the communist countries of Eastern Europe are of special interest to the student of religion because they serve more than one purpose. They function as ritual affirmations of communist ideals and commitment no less than as attempts to oust traditional religious observances—sometimes to an extent that renders them incompatible with Christian loyalty, as has been demonstrated again in East Germany. The 'confirmation' ceremony that is called *Jugendweihe* and in which the *Weihlinge* (i.e., the young boys and girls) solemnly pledge themselves to socialist solidarity has assumed such 'sacral' forms that the bishops felt that participation by Christians was impossible. Soviet publications occasionally report celebrations 'honouring the worker', e.g., when an electrical factory combines in one ceremony homage to the oldest family of workers with the 'dedication' and solemn taking of the worker's oath by the younger ones.

The Huxley quotation is taken not from the well-known evolutionist-humanist Bible, *Religion without Revelation* (1941), but from the chapter entitled 'The New Divinity' in *Essays of a Humanist* (1964). The short chapter is extremely revealing and deserves close reading. The enduring quality of 'the ritual process' (borrowing the term from Victor Turner 1969) is highlighted by the symposia and conferences devoted to it. Thus a Wenner-Gren sponsored symposium held at Burg Wartenstein in 1973 dealt with 'Ritual: Reconciliation in Change'; the follow-up symposium held in 1974 was entitled 'Secular Rituals Considered: Prolegomena Toward a Theory of Ritual, Ceremony, and Formality'.

pp. 106–9. What Marx and Engels had to say on religion is conveniently collected in Niebuhr (1957). The sentence about the 'history of multiple alienations' is taken from Birnbaum (1973) who also provides a useful bibliography at the end of his chapter. On Marx and religion there are enlightening observations in Rotenstreich (1965).

Religion as a matter of 'meaning' is discussed by Cogley (1968) in a somewhat conservative strain, and in a very different intellectual style by Bellah (1970). See also Waardenburg (1973). The subject of symbols and symbolization—both the 'forest of symbols' (to borrow another expression from Victor Turner 1967) and the trees that make up that forest—as carriers of meaning has been a major concern in modern linguistics, semiotics, psychology, theology and philosophy. As for the latter, see also Looff (1955). In connection with 'symbolic literalism' and 'historical realism', cf. also the distinction between historical and para-historical styles and references of symbolism, elaborated by Smart (1968). Chapter 2 of Smart's book is a good example of how one can deal with the myth of creation in Genesis i–ii.

The brief statement in the text to the effect that religious people are ultimately concerned not just with symbols but with their referents is meant to imply that sooner or later the ball lands in the philosopher's court. Students of religion who, like the present writer, focus on meaning, should not forget that in the last instance religion is also a matter of ontology. If the title of van Baal's interesting work (Baal 1971) expresses the major direction of present-day study of religion, it may also serve to remind us that the communication is between man and the reality intended by religion, and not merely intrasocial.

pp. 109–11. The assertion that the student of comparative religion, unlike the theologian, operates, at least ideally, from an archimedic point outside religion though inside some cultural or possibly ideological system calls for a brief excursus. There is no need here to enlarge on the trite commonplace that in social and cultural (including religious) studies the notion of 'value-free' and presuppositionless science is extremely problematic. The modern 'critical' schools harping on this point are flogging dead horses, quite apart from the fact that they seem to be critical of everything (especially 'bourgeois' sociology) except themselves. The real question relates to the consequences that should be drawn from the obvious facts, i.e., whether our inevitable limitations should be responsibly and prudently treated as necessities, or whether they should be first transformed into, and then celebrated as major virtues. The problem is especially acute in the study of religion and I deliberately avoid the expression 'Religious Studies' which figures in the names of many university departments and which gives away the ambiguity of the whole undertaking. There are indeed scholars who maintain that a commitment to a particular religion, or to religion as such, is a requirement of serious 'religious studies'. In academic terms it becomes a question of, e.g., the place of the history of religions in the university: is it in the Divinity Schools or elsewhere, and what exactly is its place in the Faculties of Theology? Since Harnack's famous lecture on the subject in 1901 ('Die Aufgabe der theologischen Fakultäten und die allgemeine Religionsgeschichte') it is almost impossible to open a volume of a theological journal without encountering a continuation of this discussion. (Two examples, chosen at random, may suffice here: the discussion between Th. P. van Baaren and H. Kraemer in the *Nederlands Theologisch Tijdschrift*, vol. 14 (1959–60), pp. 321–8 and vol. 15 (1960–1), pp. 1–10, and that between K. Rudolph and R. Panikkar in *Kairos*, vol. 9 (1967), pp. 22–42 and vol. 10 (1968), pp. 56–7 and 290–1; cf. also the article of K. Bolle in the same volume, 'Religionsgeschichtliche Forschung und theologische Impulse?'). The point I wish to make here is that religion and its study apparently play a role that cannot be compared to other cultural areas, as witnessed by the fact (pointed out by P. Berger) that many of the basic inspirations of modern sociology came from the sociology of religion. But whilst nobody would deny that there also exists a 'sociology' of music, no sociologist would claim that it sheds any light on the nature or 'essence' of music. In fact, every historian of art is deemed to have a 'positive' attitude to his subject, even though he is not required to be a practising 'virtuoso'. A musicologist need not necessarily 'like' Tchaikovsky or John Cage, but he is expected to affirm the value of music. On the other end of the scale, historians of, e.g., astrology or alchemy are not expected to 'believe in' or to have any commitments to their subject-matter (as distinct from its study). The study of religion, however, occupies any number of uneasy positions on the continuum between these two extremes.

On the place of the 'theology of religions' in the spectrum of the 'sciences' of religion, see van Baaren (1973). The theological orientation of much so-called Comparative Religion could be illustrated by a long list of books and articles whose titles begin with 'Christianity and . . .' The Barthian position is stated, among others, in the many writings of H. Kraemer (e.g., Kraemer 1956, 1961). The title of Zaehner (1964) could have served also for many of his other publications. See also Benz (1960), and for a good bibliography Benz and Nambara (1960). Brief bibliographical hints are also given by Lanczkowski (1971), pp. 165–6. Indicative of the present-day more ecumenical mood is the title of Slater (1963). A modern Catholic position is expounded by Schlette (1963). A very useful textbook of Comparative Religion bears the title *Christus und die Religionen der Erde* (F. König 1951) and concludes with a chapter by the editor 'Das Christentum und die Weltreligionen' (vol. iii, pp. 731–76). William Temple (*Readings in St. John's Gospel*, 1945, p. 10) well illustrates the imperialism of even a profoundly generous ecumenical mind: 'All that is noble in the non-Christian systems of thought, or conduct, or worship is the work of Christ upon them and within them. By the Word of God—that is to say by Jesus Christ—Isaiah and Plato, and Zoroaster, and Buddha, and Confucius conceived and uttered such truths as they declared. There is only one divine light; and every man in his measure is enlightened by it.' An extremely sophisticated version of this doctrine is presented by Panikkar (1964, 1970). After reading about 'the unknown Christ of Hinduism' all one can do is to wait for a Mahayana Buddhist to write on the unknown Buddha of Christianity; cf. my remarks (above, pp. 49–50) on the Humpty Dumpty game.

pp. 111–15. The quotation from Radhakrishnan is taken from his foreword (pp. ix–xiv) to an official publication (Publications Division, Ministry of Information and Broadcasting, Government of India) in honour of the Buddha Jayanti celebrations. (On these celebrations as a public state occasion see also D. E. Smith 1963, pp. 390 ff.) Radhakrishnan's essay was reprinted in his *Occasional Speeches and Writings 1952-1959* (1960), pp. 341–5. A more balanced view is presented, with much erudition and philosophical acumen, by Murti (1956). Unfortunately there is no full-length monograph in Western languages on the history of the notion and theory of *san-chiao*, as well as the polemical discussions concerning it. Cf. the chapter on *san-chiao* in 'The Comprehensive Discussions in the White Tiger Hall' (English ed. by Tjan Tjoe Som, in *Sinica Leidensia*, vol. 6, 1949). According to the Morohashi dictionary (*Dai-kan wa jiten*), the term was first defined at the aforementioned 'White Tiger Hall' Confucian Council (the *Po-hu t'ung*), but not with reference to the three religions. Li Shih-ch'ien (sixth century A.D.) is said to have been among the first to compare and harmonize the 'Three Teachings' of Buddhism, Taoism and Confucianism. On Li, cf. Liu Ts'un-yan, *Buddhist and Taoist Influences on Chinese Novels*, 1962 (vol. i, p. 190 f.). For examples of Confucian purist opposition to Buddhism and Taoism, cf. A. Waley, *The Life and Times of Po Chü-i*, 1949, pp. 169–71. For the Japanese, of course, *san-gyō* meant Shinto, Confucianism and Buddhism, and the great Kōbō Daishi (often called the father of Japanese syncretism) wrote a *Sangōshiki*. These and many more details and references can be found in the Morohashi dictionary. On thinking concerning *san-chiao* among Ming period intellectuals, see Wm. Th. de Bary (ed.), *Self and Society in Ming Thought*, 1970. Several important Japanese studies (e.g., by Daijō Tokiwa and Ryōon Kubota) are listed by K. Ch'en (1964) in the bibliography to chapter xviii, 'The Impact of Buddhism upon Neo-Confucianism'. Though not immediately germane to the subject, it is fitting that passing reference should be made to Waley (1939). For the quotation from Dōgen (p. 112) as well as the story about Buber (p. 115), see Werblowsky (1971). (For many of the bibliographical references in connection with *san-chiao* I am greatly indebted to Dr Anna Seidel of the Hobogirin Institute in Kyoto).

The use of the word 'vitamin' in the text is scientifically loose, and strictly speaking incorrect. 'Enzyme' would have been a more correct term, but I have opted for the more popular and hence understandable—though somewhat inaccurate—word. The long quotation on pp. 114-15 is from Heesterman (1973a).

BIBLIOGRAPHY

ADAMS, CHARLES C., 1933. *Islam and Modernism in Egypt.*

——, 1959. 'Islam in Pakistan', in Kitagawa (1959), pp. 33–58.

AHMAD, AZIZ, 1967a. *Islamic Modernism in India and Pakistan.*

——, 1967b. 'Das Dilemma von Modernismus and Orthodoxie in Pakistan', in *Saeculum*, 18, pp. 1–12.

ALI, SYED AMEER, 1922. *The Spirit of Islam: A History of the Evolution and Ideals of Islam with a Life of the Prophet.*

ANDERSON, J. N. D. AND COULSON, N. J., 1967. 'Islamic Law in Contemporary Cultural Change', *Saeculum*, 18, pp. 13–92.

BAAL, J. VAN, 1971. *Symbols for Communication: An Introduction to the Anthropological Study of Religion.*

BAAREN, TH. P. VAN, 1973. 'Science of Religion as a Systematic Discipline: Some Introductory Remarks', in van Baaren and Drijvers (1973).

BAAREN, TH. P. VAN and DRIJVERS, H. J. W. (eds.), 1973. *Religion, Culture and Methodology.*

BANTON, M. (ed.), 1966. *Anthropological Approaches to the Study of Religion.*

BAER, G. (ed.), 1971. *The 'Ulama' in Modern History. Studies in Memory of Prof. Uriel Heyd (Asian and African Studies*, vol. 7, publ. by The Israel Oriental Society).

BALJON, J. M. S., 1961. *Modern Muslim Koran Interpretation 1880-1960.*

BARNOUW, V., 1954. 'The Changing Character of a Hindu Festival', *American Anthropologist*, 56, pp. 74–86.

BARTSCH, H. (ed.), 1970. *Probleme der Entsakralarisierung.*

BASHAM, A. C., 1954. *The Wonder That Was India.*

——, 1964. 'Some Fundamental Political Ideas of Ancient India', in *Studies in Indian History and Culture*, pp. 57–71.

BECHERT, H., 1966–73. *Buddhismus, Staat und Gesellschaft* (3 vols.).

——, 1969/70. 'Theravada Buddhist Sangha: Some General Observations on Historical and Political Factors in its Development', in *Journal of Asian Studies*, 23, pp. 761–78.

——, 1973. 'Sangha, State Society, "Nation": Persistence of Traditions in Post-Traditional Buddhist Societies', in *Daedalus*, Winter 1973, pp. 85–95.

——, 1974. 'Buddhism and Mass Politics in Burma and Ceylon', in Smith, E. D., 1974, pp. 147–67.

BELL, DANIEL, 1973. *The Coming of Post-Industrial Society.*

BELLAH, ROBERT N. (ed.), 1965. *Religion and Progress in Modern Asia.*

BELLAH, ROBERT N., 1970. *Beyond Belief: Essays on Religion in a Post-Traditional World.*

BELLAH, ROBERT N. (ed.), 1973. *Emile Durkheim on Morality and Society.*

BENDIX, R., 1966–7. 'Tradition and Modernity Reconsidered', in *Comparative Studies in Society and History*, ix, pp. 292–346.

BEN-SASSON, H. H., 1971. 'Dynamic Trends in Modern Jewish Thought and Society', in Ben-Sasson and Ettinger 1971, pp. 329–44.

BEN-SASSON, H. H. and ETTINGER, S. (eds.), 1971. *Jewish Society through the Ages.*

BENZ, E., 1960. *Ideen zu einer Theologie der Religionsgeschichte.*

——, 1963. *Buddhas Wiederkehr und die Zukunft Asiens.*

BENZ, E. and NAMBARA, M., 1960. *Das Christentum und die nicht-christlichen Hochreligionen, Begegnung und Auseinandersetzung. Eine internationale Bibliographie.*

BERDIAEFF, N., 1945. 'Deux études sur Jacob Boehme', printed as introduction to the French translation of Jacob Boehme, *Mysterium Magnum.*

BERGER, PETER L., 1967. 'A Sociological View of the Secularization of Theology', in *Journal for the Scientific Study of Religion*, vi, pp. 3–16.

BIANCHI, U., 1972. 'The Definition of Religion. On the Methodology of Historical-Comparative Research', in Bianchi, Bleeker, Bausani (eds.), *Problems and Methods of the History of Religions*, pp. 15–26.

BIRNBAUM, N., 1973. 'Beyond Marx in the Sociology of Religion', in Glock and Hammond 1973.

BLACKER, C., 'Sacred and Secular in Japanese Religion' (unpublished MS.).

BLOCH, J., 1950. *Les Inscriptions d'Asoka.*

BLOCH, JOCHANAN, 1971. 'Der Zionismus als säkulares Judentum', in Schatz 1971, pp. 276–95.

BLUMENBERG, H., 1966. *Die Legitimität der Neuzeit.*

BOKSER, B., 1957. *Judaism and Modern Man. Essays in Jewish Theology.*

BOROWITZ, EUGENE B., 1970. 'Jewish Theology Faces the 1970's', in *The Annals of the American Academy of Political and Social Science*, 38, pp. 23–3.

K

BRELICH, A., 1970. 'Prolégomènes', in H. Ch. Puech (ed.), *Histoire des Religions*, vol. i, pp. 3–59.

BUBER, M., 1952. *The Eclipse of God: Studies in the Relation between Religion and Philosophy.*

——, 1958. *Paths in Utopia.*

BUSH, RICHARD C., 1970. *Religion in Communist China.*

CAPORALE, R. and GRUMELLI, A. (eds.), 1971. *The Culture of Unbelief.*

CARUS, PAUL, 1897. *Buddhism and its Christian Critics.*

CH'EN, K., 1964. *Buddhism in China.*

COBB, J. B., 1972. *Is it too late? A Theology of Ecology.*

COGLEY, JOHN, 1968. *Religion in a Secular Age: The search for Final Meaning* (with a preface by A. Toynbee).

COHEN, ARTHUR A., 1962. *The Natural and the Supernatural Jew. An Historical and Theological Introduction.*

Daedalus (Winter 1973), 1973. *Post-Traditional Societies.*

DALY, MARY, 1973. *Beyond God the Father: Toward a Philosophy of Women's Liberation.*

D'ARCY, M., 1962. *No Absent God.*

DAVIS, A. R. (ed.), 1973. *Traditional Attitudes and Modern Styles in Political Leadership* (papers presented to the 28th International Congress of Orientalists, Canberra).

DAWSON, C., 1948. *Religion and Culture.*

DEAN, VERA M., 1959. *New Patterns of Democracy in India.*

DESROCHE, M., 1962. *Marxisme et Religions.*

DUMONT, L., 1970. *Homo Hierarchicus.*

DUQUOC, CHRISTIAN, 1972. *Ambiguité des Théologies de la Sécularisation: essai critique.*

EDDINGTON, A. S., 1929. *Science and the Unseen World.*

EDWARDS, DAVID L., 1969. *Religion and Change.*

EISENSTADT, S. N., 1968. *Modernization: Protest and Change.*

——, 1973a. 'Continuity and Reconstruction of Tradition', in *Daedalus* 1973.

——, 1973b. 'The Implications of Weber's Sociology of Religion for Understanding Processes of Change in Contemporary Non-European Societies and Civilizations', in Glock and Hammond 1973 (also in *Diogenes*, 85, pp. 83–111).

——, 1973c. *Tradition, Change and Modernity.*

ELIOT, T. S., 1934. *After Strange Gods.*

——, 1939. *The Idea of a Christian Society.*

——, 1948. *Notes Towards the Definition of Culture.*

ELLWOOD, ROBERT S., 1973. *Religions and Spiritual Groups in Modern America.*

EMMET, DOROTHY, 1958. *Function, Purpose and Powers: Some Concepts in the Study of Individuals and Societies.*

FABRO, C., 1968. *God in Exile: Modern Atheism. A Study of the Internal Dynamic of Modern Atheism.*

FACKENHEIM, E., 1970. *The Quest for Past and Future: Essays in Jewish Theology.*

——, 1972. *God's Presence in History.*

FELDMAN, A. S. and MOORE, W. E., 1965. 'Are Industrial Societies Becoming Alike', in A. W. Gouldner and S. M. Miller (eds.), *Opportunities and Problems.*

FRAUWALLNER, E., 1957. 'The historical data we possess on the Person and the Doctrine of the Buddha', in *East and West*, vii, 309–12.

FREUND, WOLFGANG S., 1971. 'Religionssoziologische und sprach-strukturelle Aspekte des Entwicklungsproblems in der islamischen Welt', in *Religion and Social Change and Other Essays* (International Yearbook for the Sociology of Religion, vii, pp. 105–23).

FRIEDMANN, GEORGES, 1968. *The End of the Jewish People?*

FRYE, RICHARD N. (ed.), 1957. *Islam and the West.*

FÜRER-HAIMENDORF, C. VON, 1967. *Morals and Merit.*

GALLAGHER, CHARLES F., 1966. 'Contemporary Islam: The Straits of Secularism' (American Universities Field Staff Reports, Southwest Asia Series 15, No. 3).

GEERTZ, C. (ed.), 1963. *Old Societies and New States: The Quest for Modernity in Asia and Africa.*

GEERTZ, C., 1966. 'Religion as a Cultural System', in Banton 1966.

——, 1968. *Islam Observed.*

GEHLEN, A., 1974. 'Ende der Geschichte? Zur Lage des Menschen im Posthistoire', in Schatz 1974.

GELLNER, E., 1963. 'Sanctity, Puritanism, Secularisation and Nationalism in North Africa', in *Archives de Sociologie des Religions*, 15, pp. 71–86.

——, 1964. *Thought and Change.*

——, 1973. 'Post-Traditional Forms in Islam: The Turf and Trade, Votes and Peanuts', in *Daedalus* 1973.

GIBB, H. A. R., 1947. *Modern Trends in Islam.*

138 BIBLIOGRAPHY

GIBB, H. A. R., 1970. *Mohammedanism.*

——, 1971. 'The Reaction in the Middle East Against Western Culture', in Gibb, *Studies in the Civilization of Islam* (ed. by S. J. Shaw and W. R. Polk).

GLASENAPP, H. VON, 1922. *Der Hinduismus.*

——, 1928. 'Religiöse Reformbewegungen im heutigen Indien' (in *Morgenland*, Heft 17).

——, 1970. *Buddhism: A Non-theistic Religion.*

GLOCK, CHARLES J. (ed.), 1973a. *Religion in Sociological Perspective: Essays in the Empirical Study of Religion.*

GLOCK, C. J. and HAMMOND, PH. E. (eds.), 1973. *Beyond the Classics? Essays in the Scientific Study of Religion.*

GOGARTEN, F., 1953. *Verhängnis und Hoffnung der Neuzeit. Die Säkularisierung als theologisches Problem.*

GOLDMAN, ELIEZER, 1964. *Religion and Jewish Nationhood: Religious Issues in Israel's Political Life.*

GOLLWITZER, H., 1970. *Christian Faith and the Marxist Criticism of Religion.*

GOMBRICH, R. F., 1971. *Precept and Practice.*

GONDA, J. M., 1963. *Die Religionen Indiens* (vol. ii).

——, 1965. *Change and Continuity in Indian Religion.*

GONZALEZ-RUIS, JOSE MARIA, 1971. *Croire après Marx.*

GORDIS, R., 1955. *Judaism for the Modern Age.*

GRUNEBAUM, G. E. VON, 1957. *Problems of Muslim Nationalism.*

——, 1962, *Modern Islam.*

GUSFIELD, JOSEPH R., 1966/7. 'Tradition and Modernity: Misplaced Polarities in the Study of Social Change', in *American Journal of Sociology*, 72, pp. 351–62.

——, 1973. 'The Social Construction of Tradition: an Interactionist View of Social Change', in Davis 1973, pp. 83-104.

GUTIERREZ, G., 1972. *A Theology of Liberation.*

HARPER, MARVIN H., 1972. *Gurus, Swamis and Avatars. Spiritual Masters and their American Disciples.*

HARTMANN, W., 1969. *Was kommt nacht dem 'Tode Gottes'?*

HEER, F. and SZCZESNY, G., 1962. *Glaube und Unglaube.*

HEESTERMAN, J., 1964. 'Brahmin, Ritual and Renouncer, in *Wiener Zeitschr f. die Kunde Süd u. Ostasiens*, 8, pp. 1–31.

——, 1971a. 'Kautalya and the Ancient Indian State', in *Wiener Zeitschr f. die Kunde Süd u. Ostasiens*, 15, pp. 5–22.

——, 1971b. 'Priesthood and the Brahmin', in *Contributions to Indian Sociology*, N.S. 5, pp. 43–7 (Review Symposium on L. Dumont's *Homo Hierarchicus*).

——, 1973a. 'India and the Inner Conflict of Tradition', *Daedalus*, Winter 1973, pp. 97–113.

——, 1973b. 'Political Modernization in India', in Davis 1973, pp. 29–56.

HERBERG, W., 1955. *Protestant, Catholic, Jew*.

——, 1959. *Judaism and Modern Man—an Interpretation of Jewish Religion*.

HERTZBERG, A., 1969. *Zionism: A Historical Analysis and Reader*.

HORKHEIMER, M. and ADORNO, TH. W., 1972. *Dialectic of Enlightenment*.

HOUTART, F. and PIN, E., 1965. *The Church and the Latin-American Revolution*.

HOUTART, F. and ROUSSEAU, A., 1971. *The Church and Revolution: from the French Revolution of 1789 to the Paris riots of 1968, from Cuba to Southern Africa, from Vietnam to Latin America*.

——, 1972. *L'église et les mouvements revolutionnaires: Vietnam, Amérique Latine, Colonies Portugaises*.

HULTZSCH, E., 1925. *The Inscriptions of Asoka*.

ICE, J. L. and CAREY, J. J. (eds.), 1967. *The Death of God Debate*.

IDOWU, E. BOLAJI, 1973. *African Traditional Religions*.

IQBAL, MUHAMMAD, 1934. *The Reconstruction of Religious Thought in Islam* (second edition).

JASPERS, K., 1948. *Der philosophische Glaube*.

JENKINS, DANIEL, 1962. *Beyond Religion: The Truth and Error in 'Religionless Christianity'*.

KAMLAH, WILHELM, 1959. *Utopie, Eschatologie, Geschichtsteleologie*.

KATZ, J., 1971. 'The Jewish National Movement: A Sociological Analysis' in Ben-Sasson and Ettinger 1971, pp. 267–83.

——, 1973. *Out of the Ghetto*.

KEDOURIE, E., 1968. 'Revolutionary Nationalism in Asia and Africa', in *Government and Opposition*, iii, pp. 453–64.

KING, W. L., 1962a. *Buddhism and Christianity*.

——, 1962b. 'Buddhism and Political Power', in S. D. Browne (ed.), *Studies in Asia*.

——, 1964. *A Thousand Lives Away*.

KITAGAWA, J. M. (ed.), 1959. *Modern Trends in World Religions*.

KOEHLER, O., 1965. 'Die Zeit der "Nachgeschichte"' in *Probleme des Kulturwandels im 20. Jahrhundert* (hsg. von der Forschungsstelle für Weltzivilisation), pp. 188–207.

KOKUGAKUIN UNIVERSITY, 1967. *Continuity and Change in Shinto* (Second Conference on Shinto Studies).

KÖNIG, FRANZ (ed.), 1951. *Christus und die Religionen der Erde* (3 vols.).

KÖNIG, RENÉ, 1961. *Introduction to Durkheim, Die Regeln der Soziologische Methode.*

——, 1962. 'Die Religionssoziologie bei Emile Durkheim', in *Probleme der Religionssoziologie* (Kölner Zeitschr f. Soziologie u. Sozialpsychologie, Sonderheft 6), pp. 36–49.

KOTHARI, R., 1968. 'Tradition and Modernity Revisited', in *Government and Opposition*, iii, pp. 273–93.

KRAEMER, H., 1956. *Religion and the Christian Faith.*

——, 1961. *Christian Message in a Non-Christian World.*

KURZWEIL, B., 1953. 'The new "Canaanites" in Israel', in *Judaism*, ii, pp. 3–15.

LACROIX, JEAN, 1958. *Le sens de l'athéisme moderne.*

LANCZKOWSKI, G., 1971. *Begegnung und Wandel der Religionen.*

LAZARUS-YAFEH, H., 1971. 'Contemporary Religious Thought among the 'Ulama of Al-Azhar', in Baer 1971, pp. 211–36.

LEACH, E. R., 1973. 'Buddhism in the Post-Colonial Order in Burma and Ceylon', in *Daedalus* 1973.

LEACH, E. R. (ed.), 1968. *Dialectic in Practical Religion.*

LEEUW, G. VAN DER, 1938. *Religion in Essence and Manifestation: A Study in Phenomenology.*

LEWIS, B., 1964. *The Middle East and the West.*

——, 1970. 'Race and Colour in Islam', in *Encounter*, August 1970, pp. 18–36.

LEWY, G., 1974. 'Nasserism and Islam', in D. E. Smith 1974, pp. 253–81.

LING, T. O., 1966. *Buddha, Marx and God.*

——, 1973. *The Buddha.*

LIPSET, S. M., 1960. *Political Man.*

LOOFF, H., 1955. *Der Symbolbegriff in der neueren Religionsphilosophie und Theologie.*

LÖWITH, K., 1950. *Meaning in History: The Theological Implications of the Philosophy of History.*

——, 1952. 'Die Dynamik der Geschichte und der Historismus', *Eranos-Jahsbuch*, vol. 21.

——, 1971. 'Christentum und Geschichte', in Schatz 1971.

LÜBBE, HERMANN, 1965. *Sakularisierung: Geschichte eines ideen-politischen Begriffs.*

——, 1974. 'Vollendung der Säkulerisierung—Ende der Religion?', in Schatz 1974, pp. 145–58.

MACINNIS, DONALD E., 1972. *Religion, Policy and Practice in Communist China: A Documentary History.*

MACINTYRE, A., 1967. *Secularisation and Moral Change.*

MAHDI, M., 1959. 'Modernity and Islam', in Kitagawa 1959.

——, 1964. *Ibn Khaldun's Philosophy of History.*

MAHMASSANI, S., 1954. 'Muslims: Decadence and Renaissance', in *The Muslim World*, 44.

MALALASEKERA, G. P., 1958/9. 'Buddhism seeks the meaning of life in life itself', *The Buddhist*, 29, pp. 178–9.

——, 1973. 'Buddhism and Problems of the Modern Age', in *Voice of Buddhism* (Kuala Lumpur), 10, Nos. 3–4, pp. 6–12.

MALCOLM X., 1965. *The Autobiography of Malcolm X* (ed. by Alex Haley).

MANDELBAUM, M., 1967. Art. 'Historicism', in *The Encyclopedia of Philosophy* (ed. P. Edwards), vol. 4, pp. 22–5.

MARGUL, T., 1968. 'Present-day Worship of the Cow in India', *Numen*, xv, pp. 63–80.

MARTIN, D., 1969. *The Religious and the Secular: Studies in Secularisation.*

MARTY, MARTIN E., 1964. *The Varieties of Unbelief.*

MATTHES, J., 1967. *Religion und Gesellschaft: Einführung in die Religionssoziologie*, vol. i.

——, 1969. *Kirche und Gesellschaft: Einführung in die Religionssoziologie*, vol. ii.

MAZRUI, ALI A., 1966–7. 'Islam, Political Leadership and Economic Radicalization in Africa', in *Comparative Studies in Society and History*, ix, pp. 247–91.

MEHDEN, F. VAN DER, 1963. *Religion and Nationalism in Southeast Asia.*

MINTZ, ALAN L., 1974. *Review of H. Cox*, in *Commentary*, March 1974, pp. 94–7.

MISE EN QUESTION I, 1970. *La Sécularisation: fin ou chance du Christianisme.*

MOLTMANN, J., 1967. *Theology of Hope.*

——, 1969. *Religion, Revolution and the Future.*

MOLTMANN, J., 1972. *Theology of Play.*

——, 1973. *The Gospel of Liberation.*

MORIOKA, K., 1969. 'Contemporary Changes in Japanese Religion', in N. Birnbaum and G. Lenzer, *Sociology and Religion: A Book of Readings*, pp. 382–6.

MURRAY, J. C., 1964. *The Problem of God.*

MURTI, T. V. R., 1956. 'Buddhism and Contemporary Indian Thought', in *Revue Internationale de Philosophie*, 37, pp. 1–16.

MUS, P., 1928. 'Le Buddha paré: son origine indienne. Çakyamuni dans le Mahayanisme moyen', in *Bulletin de l'École Française d'Extrême-Orient*, vol. 28, pp. 153–278.

——, 1965. Foreword to Sarkisyanz (1965).

NASH, M. *et al.*: 1966. *Anthropological Studies in Therevada Buddhism.*

NEEDLEMAN, J., 1970. *The New Religions.*

NEUSNER, J., 1971. *Judaism in the Secular Age.*

NIEBUHR, H. RICHARD, 1929. *The Social Sources of Denominationalism.*

NIEBUHR, REINHOLD, 1957. *Marx and Engels on Religion* (with an introduction by R. Niebuhr).

NIEUWENHUIJZE, C. A. O. VAN, 1958. *Aspects of Islam in Post-Colonial Indonesia.*

NIJK, A. J., 1968. *Secularisatie: over het gebruik van een woord.*

NOVAK, M., 1965. *Belief and Unbelief.*

OBEYESEKERE, G., 1968. 'Theodicy, Sin and Salvation in a Sociology of Buddhism', in Leach 1968, pp. 7–40.

O'BRIEN, DONALD B. CRUISE, 1970. *The Mourides of Senegal.*

O'FLAHERTY, W. DONIGER, 1973. *Asceticism and Eroticism in the Mythology of Siva.*

PANIKKAR, R., 1964. *The Unknown Christ of Hinduism.*

——, 1970. *The Trinity and the Religious Experience of Man.*

——, 1973. *Worship and Secular Men.*

PARSONS, TALCOTT, 1973. 'Durkheim on Religion Revisited', in Glock and Hammond 1973.

PIEPER, J., 1963. *Belief and Faith.*

——, 1974. 'Gefährdung und Bewahrung der Tradition', in Schatz 1974, pp. 159–81.

POPE, H., 1974. *The Road East.*

POPPER, K., 1960. *The Poverty of Historicism.*

PUECH, H-CH., 1970. 'Préface' in H.-Ch Puech (ed.), *Histoire des Religions*, vol. 1, pp. vii–xxvi.

RADHAKRISHNAN, S., 1956. 'Foreword' to P. V. Bapat (gen. ed.), *2500 Years of Buddhism*, pp. ix–xiv.

RAHMAN, F., 1955. 'Internal Religious Developments in the Present Century Islam', in *Cahiers d'Histoire Mondiale*, ii, 4, pp. 862–79.

——, 1966. *Islam*.

——, 1970a. 'Islamic Modernism: Its Scope, Method and Alternatives', in *The International Journal of Middle East Studies*, i, pp. 317–33.

——, 1970b. 'Islam and the Constitutional Problem of Pakistan', in *Studia Islamica*, 32.

——, 1974. 'The Sources and Meaning of Islamic Socialism', in D. E. Smith 1974, pp. 243–58.

RENDTORFF, T., 1966. 'Zur Säkularisierungsproblematik: über die Weiterentwicklung der Kirchensoziologie zur Religionssoziologie', in *Theoretische Aspekte der Religionssoziologie* (= International Yearbook for the Sociology of Religion I).

RIEFF, PHILIP, 1961. *Freud: The Mind of the Moralist* (1st ed. 1959).

ROBERTSON, ROLAND, 1970. *The Sociological Interpretation of Religion*.

ROBINSON, I. A. T. and EDWARDS, D. L. (eds.), 1963. *The Honest to God Debate*.

RODINSON, M., 1966. *Islam et Capitalisme*.

——, 1972, *Marxisme et Monde Musulman*.

ROTENSTREICH, N., 1965. *Basic Problems of Marx's Philosophy*.

——, 1968. *Jewish Philosophy in Modern Times from Mendelssohn to Rosenzweig*.

——, 1972. *Tradition and Reality: The Impact of History on Modern Jewish Thought*.

RUDOLPH, L. I. and RUDOLPH, S. H., 1967. *The Modernity of Tradition: Political Development in India*.

RÜMKE, H. C., 1952. *The Psychology of Unbelief*.

SANDERS, TH. G., 1974. 'The New Latin American Catholicism', in D. E. Smith (1974), pp. 282–302.

SARKISYANZ, E., 1955. *Russland und der Messianismus des Orients*.

——, 1965. *Buddhist Backgrounds of the Burmese Revolution*.

SAVRAMIS, I., 1968. *Religionssoziologie*.

SCHARF, BETTY R., 1970. *The Sociological Study of Religion*.

SCHATZ, O. (ed.), 1971. *Hat die Religion Zukunft?*

——, 1974. *Was wird aus dem Menschen? Analysen und Warnungen prominenter Denker*.

SCHLETTE, H. R., 1963. *Die Religionen als Thema der Theologie*.

SCHLETTE, H. R., 1971. *Einführung in das Studium der Religionen.*

SCHMID, P., 1961. *India: Mirage and Reality.*

SCHOEPS, H. J., 1955. 'Die ausserchristlichen Religionen bei Hegel', *Zeitschrift für Religions- und Geistesgeschichte*, vii, pp. 1–34.

SCHOLEM, G., 1974. 'Jewish Theology Today', *The Center Magazine*, vol. vii, pp. 58–71.

SCHULTZ, H-J., 1964. *Konversion zur Welt.*

SCHWEID, E., 1969. 'Secularity from a Religious Point of View: Prolegomena to the Study of Rabbi Kook's Teachings', in *Petahim* No. 2 (7), Winter 1969, pp. 26–35 (in Hebrew).

SEIDENBERG, R., 1960. *The Post-Historic Man.*

SHECTER, J., 1967. *The New Face of the Buddha: the Fusion of Religion and Politics in Contemporary Buddhism.*

SHILS, E., 1971. 'Tradition', in *Comparative Studies in Society and History*, 13, pp. 122–59.

SIMON, E., 1949, 'What Price is Israel's Normalcy?', in *Commentary*, vol. 7, pp. 341–47.

——, 1953. 'Are we Israelis still Jews? The Search for Judaism in the New Society', in *Commentary*, vol. 15, pp. 357–64.

SINGER, MILTON (ed.), 1958–9. *Traditional India: Structure and Change.*

——, 1972. *When a Great Tradition Modernizes.*

SINGER, M. and COHN, B. S. (eds.), 1968. *Structure and Change in Indian Society.*

SLATER, R. L., 1963. *Can Christians Learn from Other Religions?*

SLEEPER, J. A. and MINTZ, A. L. (eds.), 1961. *The New Jews.*

SMART, N., 1968. *Secular Education and the Logic of Religion.*

SMITH, DONALD E., 1963. *India as a Secular State.*

SMITH, DONALD E. (ed.), 1966. *South Asian Politics and Religion.*

——, 1974. *Religion and Political Modernization.*

SMITH, W. C., 1957. *Islam in Modern History.*

——, 1951. *Pakistan as an Islamic State.*

——, 1963. *The Faith of Other Men.*

——, 1967. *Questions of Religious Truth.*

SÖLLE, D., 1965. *Stellvertretung: ein Kapitel Theologie nach dem 'Tode Gottes'.*

——, 1971. *Politische Theologie.*

SPERNA, WEILAND, J., 1968. *New Ways in Theology.*

SPIRO, MELFORD E., 1966. 'Religion: Problems of Definition and Explanation', in Banton 1966.

——, 1967. *Burmese Supernaturalism*.

——, 1970. *Buddhism and Society*.

SRINIVAS, M. N., 1952. *Religion and Society among the Coorgs of South India*.

——, 1962. *Caste in Modern India and Other Essays*.

——, 1968. *Social Change in Modern India*.

SWEARER, DONALD K., 1970. *Buddhism in Transition*.

SZCESNY, G., 1965. *Die Zukunft des Unglaubens*.

TAL, URIEL, 1971. 'Religious and Anti-Religious Roots of Modern Antisemitism', *Leo Baeck Memorial Lecture 14* (Leo Baeck Institute, New York).

TAMBIAH, S. J., 1968. 'The Ideology of Merit and the Social Correlates of Buddhism in a Thai Village', in Leach 1968, pp. 41–121.

——, 1970. *Buddhism and the Spirit Cults of North-east Thailand*.

——, 1973. 'The Persistence and Transformation of Tradition in Southeast Asia, with Special Reference to Thailand', in *Daedalus* 1973.

THOULESS, ROBERT H., 1940. *Conventionalization and Assimilation in Religious Movements as Problems in Social Psychology*.

TRAGER, F. (ed.), 1959. *Marxism in Southeast Asia*.

TROELTSCH, E., 1909. *Die Absolutheit des Christentums und die Religionsgeschichte*.

TURNER, BRYAN S., 1974. 'Islam, Capitalism and the Weber Theses', in *British Journal of Sociology*, xxv, pp. 230–43.

TURNER, VICTOR, 1967. *The Forest of Symbols: Aspects of Ndembu Ritual*.

——, 1969. *The Ritual Process: Structure and Anti-Structure*.

UEDA, KENJI, 1972. Chapter 'Shinto' in *Japanese Religion: A Survey for the Agency for Cultural Affairs*.

UEDA, SH., 1971. 'Der Buddhismus und das Problem der Säkularisierung. Zur gegenwärtigen geistigen Situation Japans', in Schatz 1971, pp. 255–75.

VIJAYAVARDHANA (also WIJAYAVARDHANA), D. C., 1953. *The Revolt in the Temple: composed to commemorate 2500 years of the Land, the Race, and the Faith*.

WAARDENBURG, J., 1973. 'Research on Meaning in Religion', in Baaren and Drijvers 1973, pp. 109–36.

WALEY, A., 1939. *Three Ways of Thought in Ancient China*.

WELCH, H., 1972. *Buddhism under Mao*.

WERBLOWSKY, R. J. Z., 1971. 'Universal Religion and Universalist Religion', in *International Journal for Philosophy of Religion*, ii, pp. 1–13.

WHEELIS, A., 1971. *The End of the Modern Age.*

WILSON, BRYAN, 1966. *Religion in Secular Society.*

WOLF, A. J. (ed.), 1965. *Rediscovering Judaism. Reflections on a New Theology.*

YALMAN, N., 1967. *Under the Bo Tree.*

——, 1973. 'Some Observations on Secularism in Islam: The Cultural Revolution in Turkey', in *Daedalus*, Winter 1973, pp. 139–68.

YINGER, J. MILTON, 1967. 'Pluralism, Religion and Secularization', in *Journal for the Scientific Study of Religion*, vi, pp. 17–30.

ZAEHNER, R. C., 1964. *Christianity and Other Religions.*

ZAHRNT, H., 1970. *Gott kann nicht sterben. Wider die falschen Alternativen in Theologie und Gesellschaft.*